Apocalypse &
The End Times

The Forgotten Christian and Jewish Texts That
Reveal Visions of Judgment Day and the Afterlife

A Modern Translation

Adapted for the Contemporary Reader

Various Ancient Writers

Translated by Tim Zengerink

Table of Contents

Preface - Message to the Reader

What If You Could Help Rebuild the Greatest Library in Human History?

Thousands of years ago, the Library of Alexandria stood as the crown jewel of human achievement — a sanctuary where the collected wisdom of every known civilization was gathered, preserved, and shared freely.

And then, it was lost.

Through fire, conquest, and the slow erosion of time, humanity lost not just books — but ideas, dreams, discoveries, and stories that could have changed the world forever.

Today, the Library of Alexandria lives again — and you are invited to be a part of its restoration.

Our mission is simple yet profound:

To rebuild the greatest library the world has ever known, and to translate all timeless works into every language and dialect, so that no seeker of knowledge is ever left behind again.

By joining our movement to rebuild the modern Library of Alexandria, you become part of an unprecedented mission:

- **Unlimited Access to the Greatest Audiobooks & eBooks Ever Written:**

  Instantly explore thousands of legendary works—Plato, Shakespeare, Jane Austen, Leo Tolstoy, and countless more. All instantly available to read or listen, placing a complete literary universe at your fingertips.

- **Beautiful Paperback & Deluxe Editions at Printing Cost**

  Own any title as an elegant paperback, deluxe hardcover, or stunning collectible boxset—offered to you at true printing cost, delivered straight to your door. Build your personal Library of Alexandria, crafted for beauty, built for durability, and worthy of proud display.

- **Fresh Translations for Modern Readers—in Every Language & Dialect**

  Enjoy timeless masterpieces reimagined in clear, contemporary language—no more outdated phrases or obscure references. Alongside the original versions, we're tirelessly translating these classics into every language and dialect imaginable, ensuring accessibility and understanding across cultures and generations.

- **Join a Global Renaissance of Literature & Knowledge**

  You directly support expanding our library, publishing deluxe editions at true cost, translating works into all global languages, and bringing humanity's greatest stories to people everywhere. By joining today, you're not just preserving a legacy of masterpieces; you set in motion a powerful wave of literary accessibility.

Become a Torchbearer of Knowledge.

Join us for free now at **LibraryofAlexandria.com**

Together, we will ensure that the light of human wisdom never fades again.

With gratitude and a shared love of knowledge,
The Modern Library of Alexandria Team

Visit:

www.libraryofalexandria.com

Or scan the code below:

Introduction

Lost Revelations and
the Final Destiny of the World

The question of what lies beyond death—of what fate awaits the soul, of how history will culminate, and of what divine justice ultimately looks like—has haunted humanity for millennia. From ancient prophets and seers to mystics and early apostles, many have claimed to glimpse what is hidden: the judgment to come, the realms of heaven and hell, and the cataclysmic transformation of the world in the final days. While the canonical Book of Revelation remains the most well-known biblical vision of the apocalypse, it is far from the only one. In fact, numerous apocalyptic writings once circulated widely among Jewish and Christian communities, offering rich and terrifying visions of the end times, but were later excluded from the Bible. These are the lost revelations—forgotten, suppressed, or simply neglected by history. And now, they return.

Apocalypse & The End Times gathers the most essential of these ancient prophetic texts into one modern edition. These writings—once venerated, now obscured—offer detailed, imaginative, and spiritually profound depictions of the Second Coming of Christ, the judgment of souls, the afterlife, and the divine plan for the culmination of history. They are not merely religious fantasies, but deeply symbolic expressions of a world grappling with suffering, injustice, cosmic mystery, and the hope of divine renewal. From fiery punishments to celestial thrones, from angelic interventions to the descent of the righteous into glory, these texts expand our understanding of biblical prophecy and reveal a diversity of visions that shaped early Christian and Jewish eschatology.

One of the most vivid among them is The Apocalypse of Paul, a visionary journey that guides the reader through the realms of heaven and hell. Claimed to have been revealed to the apostle Paul in a mystical ascent, this text describes with astonishing clarity the fate of souls after death—what awaits the righteous in paradise, and what torments are reserved for the wicked. It served as one of the inspirations for later medieval visions of the afterlife and influenced thinkers as far-reaching as Dante. In it, heaven is not merely a place of reward, but of spiritual transformation. Hell, meanwhile, is depicted with moral precision—each punishment corresponding to a particular sin.

Equally compelling is The Revelation of Peter, which offers an alternative and more ancient vision of the final judgment than the Book of Revelation. Written in the second century, this apocalyptic work portrays Jesus guiding Peter through terrifying scenes of divine justice. While gruesome in its imagery, it also contains notes of mercy, including the possibility of eventual forgiveness for the damned. The Revelation of Peter provides one of the earliest Christian attempts to imagine hell in graphic detail and raises profound questions about the justice and compassion of God.

The Apocalypse of Abraham, a Jewish pseudepigraphal text dating from the first or second century CE, stands out for its cosmic scale and theological depth. Here, Abraham is shown a vision of the end of the world—where the forces of evil, led by the demon Azazel, are finally defeated. This work delves into dualism, angelology, and the struggle between divine light and dark forces. It also anticipates later Christian ideas of Satan, the Antichrist, and final victory through divine intervention.

The Sibylline Oracles, a unique fusion of Jewish and early Christian prophecy composed in poetic form, offer predictions of historical events, divine wrath, and eventual redemption. These writings blend apocalyptic warnings with political critique, portraying the rise and fall of empires and the inevitable triumph of God's kingdom. They show how ancient believers interpreted global events—from the Roman Empire to natural disasters—as signs of a deeper spiritual conflict.

The Vision of Ezra, likely linked to the apocalyptic books of Esdras, presents a dialogue between Ezra and an angelic being who reveals secrets of the afterlife, the coming judgment, and the resurrection of the dead. This text focuses on divine justice, the anguish of the wicked, and the reward of the elect, speaking to communities who struggled with persecution, grief, and spiritual longing.

Finally, The Revelation of the Magi offers a very different kind of apocalypse. Rather than focusing on wrath and punishment, it presents a mystical narrative in which the Magi—those wise travelers from the East—receive a heavenly vision of Christ's divine origin and cosmic significance. This revelation, filled with starry imagery and divine light, reframes the Nativity story as a universal mystical event, accessible to those who seek truth with humility.

Visions of Judgment, Mercy, and Eternal Truth

These texts, while diverse in form and emphasis, share a common purpose: to awaken the soul, to warn the unrepentant, and to comfort the faithful with the hope that God's justice will ultimately prevail. In a world marked by suffering and uncertainty, they sought to reveal the hidden order of the cosmos and the divine plan that governs all things. For ancient readers, apocalypse was not about fear—it was about truth. The unveiling of divine reality would clarify everything: the meaning of history, the purpose of life, the fate of nations, and the condition of the soul.

The word "apocalypse" comes from the Greek word apokalypsis, meaning "unveiling" or "revelation." Contrary to modern associations with disaster and destruction, the apocalyptic tradition is fundamentally about uncovering what is hidden—bringing light to the mysteries of heaven, earth, and the afterlife. The authors of these texts believed that divine knowledge was accessible not just to prophets and saints, but to ordinary believers hungry for truth. In dreams, visions, and heavenly journeys, they saw glimpses of eternity—and they wrote them down not to terrify, but to prepare.

Why, then, were these books removed from the Bible? The reasons vary. Some were deemed too speculative or graphic. Others contradicted emerging orthodox doctrines. Still others were written too late to be accepted as apostolic. And yet, their exclusion does not diminish their value. On the contrary, these lost apocalypses remain among the most powerful expressions of faith, imagination, and divine longing ever penned.

This modern translation has been carefully adapted to retain the poetic power and spiritual depth of the originals while making them readable and relevant for contemporary audiences. Archaic terms have been clarified, theological themes explained, and contextual introductions provided where necessary. Each text invites not just reading, but contemplation—a meditation on the final things: life, death, judgment, and eternal destiny.

Whether you are a theologian, a seeker, or a lover of sacred literature, Apocalypse & The End Times will take you on a journey through forgotten heavens, hidden hells, and the burning horizon of final judgment. These are the visions that once shaped nations, inspired saints, and warned sinners. They remain as urgent and illuminating now as they were two thousand years ago.

May their light guide your path. May their warnings stir your conscience. And may their hope strengthen your faith as we all await the day when what is hidden will finally be revealed.

The Apocalypse of Abraham

Introduction

The Apocalypse of Abraham is an ancient text that expands on Abraham's story, describing his spiritual journey and the visions he received from God. Likely written during the late Second Temple period, this text gives insight into Jewish beliefs at the time, focusing on themes like divine justice, the origins of evil, and humanity's redemption.

The story follows Abraham as he rejects idolatry, receives a divine calling, and experiences powerful visions of heaven. Through rich symbolism and deep moral lessons, the text presents Abraham as both a faithful servant of God and an intercessor for humanity.

By including this text in the collection, readers can gain a deeper understanding of Abraham's importance in religious history and the broader spiritual ideas of ancient Judaism.

The Apocalypse of Abraham

Abraham was known for his kindness, fairness, and generosity. He lived near a place called Dria the Black, at a crossroads where many travelers passed through. He welcomed everyone—rich or poor, kings or commoners, strong or weak. No matter who they were, Abraham treated them with kindness because he was a good and just man who loved people.

One day, the Lord called the archangel Michael and said, "Go to my servant Abraham and remind him that his time on earth is coming to an end. I have blessed him greatly, making his descendants as countless as the stars in the sky and the sand on the shore. He has lived a life full of goodness and generosity. Now, his time has come."

Michael, who sat before the Lord, left heaven and went to find Abraham in Dria the Black. When he arrived, he saw Abraham working in the field with his servants and some young men. The archangel approached him and said, "Greetings, honored father, chosen one of the Lord, beloved friend of the King of Heaven."

Abraham replied, "Greetings to you, mighty one of God's army! You are more radiant than any man I have ever seen. Tell me, young man, where do you come from, and why do you shine so brightly?"

Michael answered, "Righteous Abraham, I come from the Great City. The Great King has sent me to His chosen friend to tell him to prepare himself, for the Lord is calling him."

Abraham nodded and said, "Very well. Let us go back to my home." Then he called his servants and said, "Go to the field and bring two of my horses. Prepare them so I may ride one, and my guest may ride the other."

But Michael replied, "Do not bring the horses. I do not ride animals with four legs. Let us walk together, righteous one."

As they walked, they passed by a tall and sturdy cypress tree. Suddenly, the tree cried out, "The Lord calls you, Abraham!" But Abraham remained silent, unsure if the angel had heard it.

When they reached Abraham's home, they sat down. Isaac, Abraham's son, saw the angel and said to his mother, Sarah, "Look at the man sitting with my father. He does not look like any ordinary person."

Isaac ran to the angel, bowed before him, and the angel blessed him, saying, "May God give you all the blessings He has given to your father and mother."

Abraham turned to Isaac and said, "Bring a basin and fill it with water so we can wash our guest's feet."

Isaac ran to the well, filled a basin, and brought it back. As Abraham washed the angel's feet, he sighed deeply and began to cry. Seeing his father weep, Isaac also started to cry, and their tears fell together. The angel, moved by their sadness, wept as well. As his tears fell into the basin, they turned into precious stones.

When Abraham saw this, he gathered the jewels and kept their meaning in his heart.

Then Abraham told his son, "Go prepare two beds carefully. Set candles in the candlesticks, lay out the table, light incense, and spread fragrant herbs on the floor so the room smells sweet. Light seven candles so that we may celebrate this guest, who is greater than any man and mightier than kings."

Isaac did everything as his father instructed.

Abraham and the angel went into the prepared room. They sat down on separate beds with a table of food between them. Then the angel returned to the Lord and said, "Lord, I have seen Abraham's righteousness, kindness, and incredible strength. I cannot bring myself to tell him about his approaching death because I have never met anyone like him on earth."

The Lord replied, "Go back to my friend Abraham. Eat the food he has prepared, and I will send My Spirit to his son Isaac. In a dream, I will reveal to him that his father's time is near. You will interpret the dream so that Abraham may understand that his time has come."

The archangel said, "Lord, heavenly beings do not eat or drink. How can I sit and eat with Abraham?"

The Lord replied, "Do not worry. I will send spirits to make the food disappear from your hands and mouth, as if you were eating. This will bring joy to Abraham and his family. Also, explain Isaac's dream so they understand what is about to happen."

The archangel returned to Abraham, and they ate together. As usual, Abraham said a prayer before the meal. After eating, they prayed again and then rested on their beds.

Isaac turned to his father and said, "I want to stay here and listen to our guest."

But Abraham replied, "No, my son. Go to bed and rest. We must not trouble our guest."

Isaac obeyed, received his father's blessing, and went to his room.

Later that night, Isaac had a dream that frightened him. He ran to his father's room, where Abraham was still with the archangel, and cried, "Father Abraham, please open the door! Let me hold you before they take you away from me!"

Abraham got up and opened the door. Isaac ran inside, embraced his father, and wept loudly. Abraham also wept, and when the archangel saw them, he wept too.

Abraham gently asked Isaac, "My dear son, tell me what you saw in your dream that has upset you so much."

Isaac replied, "I saw the sun and the moon resting on my head, shining brightly in all directions. At first, I was happy, but then the heavens opened, and a glowing man came down. He removed the sun from my head and took it to heaven. Then he did the same with the moon. I begged him, 'Please, do not take them away from me!' But he said, 'Let them go. The Lord of Heaven has called for them.' Although they left some of their light behind, I felt heartbroken."

Abraham sighed and said, "The sun you saw, and the glowing man from heaven, must mean that my time to leave has come." He then turned to the angel and said, "Oh, how amazing! But I fear you are the one who has come to take my soul from me."

The archangel replied, "I am the angel sent to bring you news of your passing. You will go to the Lord as promised in your covenant."

Abraham answered, "Now I understand that you are here to take my soul, but I will not go willingly!"

The angel returned to the Lord and reported everything that had happened, including Abraham's refusal, saying, "He will not surrender."

The Lord said to the archangel, "Go back to my friend Abraham and remind him: I am the Lord, his God, who led him to the Promised Land. I blessed him with descendants as countless as the sand on the shore and the stars in the sky. How dare he resist me? Does he not know that since the time of Adam and Eve, all people have died? Kings, ancestors, and all of humanity have faced death because no one is immortal.

"But I have not sent him sickness, suffering, or the grim reaper to take him away. Instead, I sent my archangel Michael with this message so Abraham could prepare himself. Why does he resist my messenger? Does he not know I could send the angel of death, whose presence he could not endure?"

The archangel returned to Abraham and repeated the Lord's words. Abraham wept and said, "Mighty angel of heaven, though I am a sinner, you have honored me. Please grant me one last request. The Lord has always answered my prayers and given me what I asked for. I know I cannot escape death, but before I die, let me see all the people of the earth and their deeds while I am still alive. After that, I will surrender myself completely."

The archangel returned to heaven and told the Lord about Abraham's request.

The Lord said, "Place my servant Abraham in the chariot of the cherubim and bring him up to heaven."

Then sixty angels prepared the chariot. Abraham was lifted up on the clouds. As he traveled, he saw another chariot behind him and groups of people below.

In one area, he saw people committing terrible sins and cried out, "Lord, let the earth open and swallow them!"

In another place, he saw people stealing and harming others and shouted, "Lord, send fire from heaven to destroy them!"

Fire came down and consumed them.

A voice from heaven commanded, "Take Abraham away from this sight so he will not see the people any longer. If he continues watching their sins, he will destroy them all. But I do not wish for anyone to perish. I want the wicked to repent and live. Take Abraham to the first gate of heaven so he may witness the final judgment and humble himself even more."

The archangel turned Abraham's chariot and brought him to the first gate of heaven. There, he saw two paths—one narrow and difficult, the other wide and easy.

On the narrow path, only a few souls were walking, each guided by an angel.

On the wide path, there were many souls, but they looked wounded

14

and suffering, being led by different beings.

Then Abraham noticed a powerful figure sitting on a golden throne. Sometimes, the figure wept, pulling at his hair and beard when he saw the many souls on the wide path. Other times, he rejoiced when he saw the few souls walking the narrow path.

Abraham turned to the archangel and asked, "Who is this man who switches between sorrow and joy?"

The archangel answered, "This is Adam, the first man, created to bring beauty to the world. He rejoices when he sees souls on the narrow path because it leads to life. But when he sees so many souls on the wide path, which leads to destruction, he mourns deeply."

As they spoke, two angels arrived, bringing countless souls before Adam. Some were sent down the narrow path, while others were turned away.

Then Abraham saw another golden throne at a large gateway. It shined like fire, and a man sat on it, resembling the Son of God. In front of him was a massive table, and two angels stood beside him.

One angel held a set of scales, and the other held a scroll listing all the temptations and sins of humanity. The man judged each soul, deciding their fate.

The angel on the right recorded virtues, while the angel on the left noted sins. Some souls were condemned, others were set free, and a few were placed in the middle.

Abraham asked the archangel, "What is this I see before me?"

The angel replied, "These are the judges, and they pass judgment on every soul that comes before them."

Abraham watched as one soul was brought forward.

An angel said, "This soul has an equal number of good and bad deeds. Erase its record, for it will neither be saved nor condemned. Place it in the middle."

Abraham then asked, "Who are these judges and the glowing angels surrounding them?"

The archangel said, "Lord, heavenly beings do not eat or drink. How can I sit and eat with Abraham?"

The Lord replied, "Do not worry. I will send spirits to make the food disappear from your hands and mouth, as if you were eating. This will bring joy to Abraham and his family. Also, explain Isaac's dream so they understand what is about to happen."

The archangel returned to Abraham, and they ate together. As usual, Abraham said a prayer before the meal. After eating, they prayed again and then rested on their beds.

Isaac turned to his father and said, "I want to stay here and listen to our guest."

But Abraham replied, "No, my son. Go to bed and rest. We must not trouble our guest."

Isaac obeyed, received his father's blessing, and went to his room.

Later that night, Isaac had a dream that frightened him. He ran to his father's room, where Abraham was still with the archangel, and cried, "Father Abraham, please open the door! Let me hold you before they take you away from me!"

Abraham got up and opened the door. Isaac ran inside, embraced his father, and wept loudly. Abraham also wept, and when the archangel saw them, he wept too.

Abraham gently asked Isaac, "My dear son, tell me what you saw in your dream that has upset you so much."

Isaac replied, "I saw the sun and the moon resting on my head, shining brightly in all directions. At first, I was happy, but then the heavens opened, and a glowing man came down. He removed the sun from my head and took it to heaven. Then he did the same with the moon. I begged him, 'Please, do not take them away from me!' But he said, 'Let them go. The Lord of Heaven has called for them.' Although they left some of their light behind, I felt heartbroken."

Abraham sighed and said, "The sun you saw, and the glowing man from heaven, must mean that my time to leave has come." He then turned to the angel and said, "Oh, how amazing! But I fear you are the one who has come to take my soul from me."

The archangel replied, "I am the angel sent to bring you news of your passing. You will go to the Lord as promised in your covenant."

Abraham answered, "Now I understand that you are here to take my soul, but I will not go willingly!"

The angel returned to the Lord and reported everything that had happened, including Abraham's refusal, saying, "He will not surrender."

The Lord said to the archangel, "Go back to my friend Abraham and remind him: I am the Lord, his God, who led him to the Promised Land. I blessed him with descendants as countless as the sand on the shore and the stars in the sky. How dare he resist me? Does he not know that since the time of Adam and Eve, all people have died? Kings, ancestors, and all of humanity have faced death because no one is immortal.

"But I have not sent him sickness, suffering, or the grim reaper to take him away. Instead, I sent my archangel Michael with this message so Abraham could prepare himself. Why does he resist my messenger?

Does he not know I could send the angel of death, whose presence he could not endure?"

The archangel returned to Abraham and repeated the Lord's words. Abraham wept and said, "Mighty angel of heaven, though I am a sinner, you have honored me. Please grant me one last request. The Lord has always answered my prayers and given me what I asked for. I know I cannot escape death, but before I die, let me see all the people of the earth and their deeds while I am still alive. After that, I will surrender myself completely."

The archangel returned to heaven and told the Lord about Abraham's request.

The Lord said, "Place my servant Abraham in the chariot of the cherubim and bring him up to heaven."

Then sixty angels prepared the chariot. Abraham was lifted up on the clouds. As he traveled, he saw another chariot behind him and groups of people below.

In one area, he saw people committing terrible sins and cried out, "Lord, let the earth open and swallow them!"

In another place, he saw people stealing and harming others and shouted, "Lord, send fire from heaven to destroy them!"

Fire came down and consumed them.

A voice from heaven commanded, "Take Abraham away from this sight so he will not see the people any longer. If he continues watching their sins, he will destroy them all. But I do not wish for anyone to perish. I want the wicked to repent and live. Take Abraham to the first gate of heaven so he may witness the final judgment and humble himself even more."

The archangel turned Abraham's chariot and brought him to the first gate of heaven. There, he saw two paths—one narrow and difficult, the other wide and easy.

On the narrow path, only a few souls were walking, each guided by an angel.

On the wide path, there were many souls, but they looked wounded and suffering, being led by different beings.

Then Abraham noticed a powerful figure sitting on a golden throne. Sometimes, the figure wept, pulling at his hair and beard when he saw the many souls on the wide path. Other times, he rejoiced when he saw the few souls walking the narrow path.

Abraham turned to the archangel and asked, "Who is this man who switches between sorrow and joy?"

The archangel answered, "This is Adam, the first man, created to bring beauty to the world. He rejoices when he sees souls on the narrow path because it leads to life. But when he sees so many souls on the wide path, which leads to destruction, he mourns deeply."

As they spoke, two angels arrived, bringing countless souls before Adam. Some were sent down the narrow path, while others were turned away.

Then Abraham saw another golden throne at a large gateway. It shined like fire, and a man sat on it, resembling the Son of God. In front of him was a massive table, and two angels stood beside him.

One angel held a set of scales, and the other held a scroll listing all the temptations and sins of humanity. The man judged each soul, deciding their fate.

The angel on the right recorded virtues, while the angel on the left noted sins. Some souls were condemned, others were set free, and a few were placed in the middle.

Abraham asked the archangel, "What is this I see before me?"

The angel replied, "These are the judges, and they pass judgment on every soul that comes before them."

Abraham watched as one soul was brought forward.

An angel said, "This soul has an equal number of good and bad deeds. Erase its record, for it will neither be saved nor condemned. Place it in the middle."

Abraham then asked, "Who are these judges and the glowing angels surrounding them?"

The Sibylline Oracles

Introduction

The Sibylline Oracles are a collection of ancient prophetic writings created over several centuries. They combine ideas from Greek, Jewish, and early Christian traditions. These oracles are linked to the Sibyls, legendary prophetesses of the ancient world. Written in Greek poetry, they were used to spread religious and political messages. Their long history reflects the mix of different cultures and beliefs in the Mediterranean from ancient times to the early Middle Ages.

The idea of the Sibyl originally came from ancient Greece, where people believed that one prophetess revealed divine messages. Over time, different Sibyls appeared across the Mediterranean, including the famous Cumaean Sibyl, who, according to Roman mythology, advised the hero Aeneas. The Sibylline Oracles are not the same as the original Roman Sibylline Books, which were official prophetic texts lost long ago. Instead, the surviving oracles are a mix of writings from different sources, created between the 2nd century BCE and the 7th century CE. They combine Greek and Roman myths with Jewish, Gnostic, and early Christian ideas, forming a unique collection of prophecy.

The oracles contain 12 main books, totaling over 4,000 lines. The Sibyl speaks in the first person and mostly describes the future. The content varies, including visions of the end of the world, moral lessons, and prophecies about final judgment. Some sections use acrostics, where the first letters of each line spell out hidden messages, showing the detailed writing style of the authors.

These oracles were written during times of political and religious struggles. Jewish writers used the Sibyl's voice to challenge oppressive rulers and promote belief in one God, blending Jewish ideas into the prophecies. As Christianity spread, Christian writers added references to Jesus and Christian teachings, reshaping the oracles to support their religious messages. This mix of traditions made the oracles useful for connecting with pagan audiences, giving Christian beliefs more credibility by presenting them through a respected prophetic figure.

The oracles were passed down through handwritten copies from the 14th to the 16th centuries. These manuscripts show signs of editing over time, and scholars have grouped them based on content and history. Early Christian leaders, such as Theophilus of Antioch, Clement of Alexandria, and Lactantius, often quoted the oracles, showing their influence in early Christian writings.

The Sibylline Oracles played an important role in religious thought and culture. In ancient times, Jewish and Christian scholars used them to support their faith, portraying the Sibyl as a pagan prophetess who predicted monotheism and Christianity. During the Renaissance, interest in the oracles returned, inspiring artists and writers to explore classical ideas and wisdom. Today, they are still studied for their blend of different cultural stories and their influence on prophetic and apocalyptic traditions.

The Sibylline Oracles represent the rich exchange of ideas between different cultures and religions in the ancient Mediterranean. They show how Jewish and Christian communities adapted existing pagan traditions to spread their beliefs. As a result, these writings provide valuable insight into the blending of religious ideas, the early development of Christianity, and humanity's ongoing fascination with prophecy and divine messages.

Book 1.

I will tell the story of humans from the very first to the very last. I will explain what has happened before, what is happening now, and what will happen in the future because of people's wrongdoing.

First, God wants me to explain how the world was made. Listen carefully and remember what I say, so you don't forget the commands of the most powerful King—the one who created everything by simply saying, "Let there be," and it happened.

He made the earth and placed it near the deep, dark pit below. He gave light to the world, lifted the sky high, spread the shining sea, and filled the heavens with countless bright stars. He covered the earth with plants, mixed rivers into the seas, and blended the air with gentle winds and clouds full of water. Then, he created living things—fish for the oceans, birds for the skies, wild animals for the forests, and snakes that crawl on the ground. Everything that exists now, he made with his words. It was all done quickly and perfectly because he is powerful and sees everything from above.

After creating the world, he made something special—a living being, a human, designed in his own image. He was beautiful and godlike. God placed him in a wonderful garden, giving him work to do so he could care for it. But the man, alone in this paradise, wanted someone to talk to. He prayed for a companion, someone like him.

So, God took a bone from his side and made a woman, Eve, to be his wife. She lived with him in the garden. When the man saw her, he was filled with happiness and amazement because she was a perfect match for him. They lived without shame, not even needing clothes, because their hearts were pure and free from evil.

God gave them one rule—not to eat from a certain tree. But a cunning serpent tricked them into disobeying. He convinced Eve to eat the forbidden fruit, and she gave some to the man. He listened to her and forgot God's command. Because they disobeyed, they brought suffering upon themselves instead of the good life they had.

Right away, they realized they were naked and, feeling ashamed, made clothes out of fig leaves. God was angry and sent them out of paradise to live in the world as mortals. Since they did not listen, they could no longer stay in the perfect land.

With sadness and tears, they stepped out into the world. God told them to work hard, to grow their family, and to provide for themselves through labor. From then on, survival would take effort.

As punishment, God made the serpent crawl on its belly in the dirt forever, and he put hatred between the snake and humans.

People learned to protect themselves from danger, always watching out for threats. But danger was close—both from poisonous snakes and from wicked people. Over time, the human race grew, just as God had commanded. Many generations passed, and countless people filled the earth. They built homes, created cities, and constructed strong walls with great skill. Life was long and enjoyable in those days. People didn't suffer from sickness and hardships as they do now. Instead, when their time came, they passed away peacefully, like falling into a deep sleep. These were strong, fortunate people whom God, the eternal ruler, deeply loved.

However, even they made mistakes. Foolishness led them astray. They disrespected their parents, ignored their relatives, and betrayed their own family members. Some became violent and killed others, bringing war upon themselves. Because of their evil actions, a great disaster came from heaven and wiped them out. Their lives ended, and the underworld took them in. Since Adam was the first to experience death, this place of the dead became known as Hades, and from then on, every person born on earth would eventually go there.

Even in Hades, the first people were honored because they had been the original race of mankind. But after they were gone, God created another group of people. These were clever and hardworking, focused on creating beautiful things and using their wisdom. They learned many skills—farming, carpentry, sailing, and even studying the stars. Some practiced healing with medicines, while others explored magic and different kinds of knowledge. These people were highly intelligent, always thinking and inventing, and they were strong in both body and mind.

But despite their abilities, they, too, eventually fell into darkness. Because of their actions, they were punished and thrown into a terrible place, locked away in chains. There, they suffered in an unending, fiery prison.

After them, another race appeared—fierce and arrogant. These people were cruel and constantly at war, fighting and killing one another. From them came yet another generation, the fourth race of humans. They were even worse—full of anger, violence, and wickedness. They had no respect for God or for each other, and their reckless ways led them to endless wars and bloodshed. Many were sent into the depths of the underworld because of their crimes. Others angered God so much that he cast them into the deepest, darkest pit beneath the earth, a place of eternal punishment.

But the worst was still to come. A final race of people emerged—more wicked than all those before them. They were brutal, spoke harshly, and acted without mercy. They did so much evil that they were beyond saving.

Among them, only one man stood out—Noah. He was honest, righteous, and devoted to doing good. Because of this, God spoke to him from heaven, saying, "Noah, do not be afraid. Tell the people to change their ways so they can be saved. But if they refuse to listen, I will destroy them all."

"I will send a great flood to cover the earth. Now, hurry and build a strong, waterproof house made of sturdy wooden planks. I will give you wisdom, skill, and the knowledge you need to measure and build it correctly. I will take care of everything so that you and those with you will be safe.

I am the one who exists above all things. Look inside your heart, and you will understand. I cover myself with the sky, surround myself with the sea, and the earth is beneath my feet. The air flows around me, and the stars move in harmony around me.

My name has nine letters and four syllables. The first three parts each have two letters, and the last part holds the rest. The sum of its numbers equals twice eighty plus three times thirty, plus seven. If you understand who I am, do not ignore my teachings."

When Noah heard these words, he was overcome with fear. But he understood what had to be done. He turned to the people and spoke:

"O people filled with greed and madness, do you think your wicked deeds go unnoticed? God sees everything. He has sent me to warn you so that you do not perish. Turn away from your evil ways. Stop fighting and spilling the blood of others. Do not stain the land with violence.

Respect the great and powerful Creator, who lives in the heavens. He is kind—ask him for mercy, not just for yourselves, but for the cities, the world, the animals, and the birds. Pray for his kindness.

If you do not change, the earth will be destroyed by a mighty flood.

When that time comes, you will cry out in terror, but it will be too late. The sky will become wild and chaotic, and the wrath of God will come down upon you. If you refuse to turn back now, nothing will stop the punishment that is coming. Do not harm one another anymore—choose to live righteously."

But when the people heard this, they laughed and mocked Noah. They called him crazy and ignored his warning.

Noah spoke again: "You are miserable and full of evil. You have no sense of honor and only care about satisfying your own greed. You are liars, thieves, and adulterers. You speak carelessly and disrespectfully, showing no fear of God's power. Your punishment has been decided, and it will come upon you soon.

You laugh now, but you will not laugh when the great flood arrives. This world, filled with people who have turned away from God, will be wiped out in a single night. Everything—men, cities, and buildings—will be torn apart and destroyed. The entire human race will vanish. How will I mourn for you when I am shut inside my wooden house? How can I cry when the waters rise and swallow everything?

When the flood comes, the earth will float, the mountains will float, and even the sky will seem to float. Everything will be covered in water, and life as you know it will end. The winds will stop, and a new age will begin.

Phrygia, you will be the first to rise from the waters. You will be the first land where a new generation of people will grow, a fresh start for humanity."

Even after Noah warned them, the people refused to listen. Then, the Almighty appeared once more and said:

"Noah, the time has come to do everything I told you. The people have not changed. They continue to live in wickedness, just like those before them. Now, go inside with your family. Bring in the animals, birds, and creatures I have chosen to survive. I will guide them to you and make them willing to enter."

Noah obeyed. He called his family, and they all entered the wooden house. Then, the animals followed, just as God had commanded.

Noah made sure to bring everything God commanded onto the ark. Once the door was sealed tightly in place, God's plan began to unfold.

Dark clouds gathered, covering the sky and blocking out the sun, moon, and stars. The heavens grew dark as loud thunder shook the earth, and flashes of lightning lit up the sky. The winds howled, and suddenly, water poured from above in powerful torrents. At the same time, water gushed up from the ground, rising higher and higher until the entire earth was submerged.

The ark floated on the vast waters, tossed about by the raging waves. Fierce winds battered it, but it stayed afloat, cutting through the churning sea. The sound of crashing water echoed all around. As the rain poured endlessly, Noah watched and waited, following God's guidance. He had seen enough of the endless ocean and longed for solid ground again.

After many days of rain, Noah decided to check if the waters were receding. He unfastened a small opening in the ark's wall and peered outside. All he could see was water stretching in every direction. The sight of it made his heart tremble.

Then, after a long time, the rain stopped. The sky, tired of pouring water, finally began to clear. The sun appeared, its light weak and pale, shining over the flooded world. Though Noah tried to stay strong, the sight filled him with fear.

To see if land had reappeared, he sent out a dove. It flew over the endless water but found nowhere to rest, so it returned to him. The earth was still completely covered. He waited patiently and sent the dove out again after a few more days. This time, it returned with an olive branch in its beak—a sign that dry land was near. Hope filled Noah and his family, as they knew the flood was finally receding.

Then Noah released a black-winged bird, which flew off and did not return. This meant that land was close enough for creatures to survive.

The ark, after drifting for so long, finally came to rest on a narrow strip of land. It had landed on a tall mountain in Phrygia, called Ararat. This was the place where those who survived the flood would begin again. From this mountain flowed the great river Marsyas.

Once the waters had completely dried, God spoke to Noah again:

"Noah, my faithful servant, step out of the ark with your family. Bring out all the animals so they may spread across the earth once more. Multiply and fill the world. Live with justice and treat each other with kindness. A time will come when all people will be judged, but for now, rebuild the world."

Noah obeyed. He and his family stepped out onto dry land, along with the animals, birds, and every living thing that had been in the ark.

Noah, the most righteous among them, had spent forty-one days on the waters, trusting in God's plan. When he finally set foot on solid ground, a new chapter for humanity began.

This new generation, the sixth since the beginning of mankind, was golden—the best of them all. It was called the Heavenly Age because God cared for them in a special way.

I, too, was part of this new world, saved from disaster. Along with my husband, my brothers-in-law, my stepfather, my stepmother, and their wives, we endured the storm and survived the great flood.

Soon, amazing things would happen. A special flower would bloom on the fig tree, marking the beginning of a new era. Three just and noble kings would rule, each dividing the land fairly and governing with wisdom.

The earth would flourish once more, producing abundant food without effort. The people of this time would live long, free from sickness and suffering. When their time came, they would pass away peacefully, as if falling into a deep sleep. In the afterlife, they would be honored for the good lives they had lived.

The blessed ones, the fortunate heroes, were given wisdom by the Lord of Heaven. He guided them and shared his plans with them. Even in death, they would still be blessed.

But after them, another powerful race would rise—the Titans. These giants would be taller and stronger than any before them, and they would all speak the same language, just as the first humans did. However, their pride would lead to their downfall. They would become so arrogant that they would try to fight against the heavens themselves.

In response, the great ocean would flood over them, drowning the land. But despite his anger, God would hold back his full wrath, keeping his promise never to destroy the world with a flood again.

When God, the ruler of the skies, finally calms the stormy waters and sets their limits with shores and cliffs, something extraordinary will happen. A child of God will come into the world, born as a human.

His name will contain four vowels and two repeating consonants. If you add the numerical value of his letters, the total will be 888. If you understand this, you will know that he is the Christ, the Son of the eternal God.

He will not destroy God's law but will fulfill it. He will carry God's image and teach the world. Wise men will bring him gifts of gold, myrrh, and incense, and all of these things will come to pass.

One day, a voice will cry out in the wilderness, telling people to change their ways. This voice will call on everyone to purify themselves with water and turn away from evil so they may live righteously. But a cruel ruler, deceived by a dance, will order this voice to be silenced forever.

Then, a great sign will appear. A precious stone from Egypt will cause the Hebrew people to stumble, yet it will guide other nations to unity. Through him, people will come to know the one true God and find the path to salvation. He will show chosen people the way to eternal life, but those who reject him will face eternal fire.

This child of God will heal the sick and give hope to those who believe in him. The blind will see, the crippled will walk, the deaf will hear, and the mute will speak. He will cast out demons, bring the dead back to life, and walk on water. In a deserted place, he will feed five thousand people with just five loaves of bread and a single fish. Afterward, twelve baskets will be filled with the leftovers, a sign of hope for many.

But Israel will not understand. They will be blinded by their own stubbornness, refusing to listen. And when God's anger falls upon them, they will lose their faith because they rejected and killed the Son of God.

In their cruelty, they will strike him, spit on him, and offer him bitter gall and vinegar instead of food and drink. Their hearts will be filled with wickedness, unable to see the truth, trapped in darkness like blind moles or venomous snakes.

When he stretches out his hands to embrace all, they will place a crown of thorns on his head and pierce his side with a spear. As a sign of this great injustice, the sun will be darkened, and midday will turn into night for three hours. The great temple of Solomon will shake, and he will descend into the depths of the underworld, bringing the promise of resurrection to the dead.

After three days, he will rise again, showing himself to the people and teaching them. Then, he will ascend to heaven, leaving behind his teachings as a new covenant for the world.

Through him, a new people will grow—those who follow the law of the Almighty. Wise leaders will guide them, but eventually, prophecy will come to an end.

Later, when the Hebrews face the consequences of their actions, a Roman king will take away their gold and silver. Kingdoms will continue to rise and fall, bringing suffering to many. Those who become too proud and unjust will face a great downfall.

When Solomon's temple is destroyed by armored invaders, the Hebrew people will be scattered, wandering without a home. They will mix among other nations, bringing hardship upon themselves and others. The cities will suffer from violence and destruction, crying out in sorrow. And as the world turns further from righteousness, God's wrath will come upon the people for the evil they have done.

Book 2.

As I prayed, God held back my words for a time, but then he placed his divine message in my heart again. His voice flows through me, and though I don't fully understand everything I say, he guides me to speak the truth.

One day, the earth will shake with violent storms, fierce lightning, and terrifying thunder. Wild animals like jackals and wolves will grow more aggressive, and there will be terrible bloodshed. People, cattle, horses, sheep, and goats will perish. Fields will be abandoned, crops will fail, and famine will spread. Many people will be sold into slavery, and even sacred temples will be looted.

Then, a new generation will rise—the tenth race of humanity. During this time, God will put an end to idol worship and shake the mighty city of Rome, which stands on seven hills. Its vast wealth will be burned away by fire. Signs will appear in the sky, warning of the destruction to come.

The world will fall into chaos. People will turn against each other in anger, and war will rage everywhere. God will send plagues, famine, and storms to punish those who judge unfairly and act without justice. So many will die that if someone were to find another living person, they would be shocked.

But after this suffering, God will save those who are faithful. Peace and wisdom will fill the earth once more. The land will become fertile again, producing plenty of food without division or slavery. The ports and harbors will be open to everyone, and wickedness will disappear.

Then, God will show the people a great sign. A bright star will shine in the sky like a glowing crown, remaining for many days. It will be a signal for a great challenge, a test for those who seek victory. This challenge will be open to everyone, and those who succeed will be remembered forever. No one will be able to buy their way to victory with money—only those who are worthy will win.

Christ, who is pure and just, will judge each person fairly. He will reward those who stayed faithful, and he will grant an eternal prize to the martyrs who gave their lives for the truth. Those who lived righteously, remaining loyal in marriage and avoiding corruption, will receive his blessings and eternal hope.

Every soul is a gift from God, and no one should stain it with wickedness. Do not seek wealth through dishonest means, but be content with what you have. Do not take what belongs to someone else. Speak honestly and value the truth.

Do not worship false gods, but honor the one true and everlasting God. Respect your parents, fulfill your responsibilities, and avoid making unfair judgments. Do not cast out the poor or treat people differently based on appearances—if you judge unfairly, God will judge you in the same way.

Never give false testimony; always speak the truth. Stay pure and protect the love shared between people. Be fair in your dealings, and do not tip the scales dishonestly—always measure things correctly. Never swear falsely, for God despises lies.

Do not accept gifts that come from evil actions. Never steal what is meant for others, for it brings a curse across generations. Avoid sinful desires, do not spread lies, and do not take another's life.

Pay workers their wages, and do not mistreat those who are poor. Help orphans, widows, and those in need. Speak wisely and keep secrets in confidence. Never do wrong, and do not support those who act unjustly.

Give to the poor without delay—do not tell them to return another day. Share your food with those in need, and be generous, offering help with a willing heart.

Whoever gives to the poor is lending to God. Kindness and mercy will save a person when the time of judgment comes. God values mercy more than sacrifices.

Give clothes to those who have none, share your food with the hungry, and provide shelter for those without a home. Help those who are lost, guide the blind, and show compassion to those who have suffered misfortune. Life is uncertain, and no one knows what tomorrow will bring. If someone has fallen, offer them a helping hand. Defend those who have no one to stand up for them.

Everyone experiences hardships because life is always changing. Wealth is temporary, so if you have riches, use them to help others. Share what God has given you with those in need. Though all people are born into the same world, life is not always fair.

If you see someone struggling, do not mock them. Do not be harsh to those who have made mistakes. A person's true character is revealed after they are gone—whether they lived justly or not will be decided at the final judgment.

Do not dull your mind with too much wine, and avoid drinking excessively. Do not consume blood, and do not eat food that has been sacrificed to idols. Do not take up a sword unless it is for protection, and even then, it is better not to use it at all. If you kill, even in battle, your hands will be stained.

Respect your neighbor's property, and do not take what is not yours. Boundaries exist for a reason, and trespassing leads to trouble. It is good to have honest wealth, but money gained unfairly is worthless in the end. Do not harm the crops of others, and treat strangers with the same respect as your own people.

All people should treat each other with kindness because no one truly owns the land forever. Do not wish for great wealth. Instead, pray for a simple and honest life. Greed is the root of all evil. Do not crave gold or silver, as they lead people into temptation and destruction. Money has caused wars, robberies, and even families to turn against each other. Because of it, children have betrayed their parents, and siblings have fought among themselves.

Do not deceive others or plot against your friends. Be honest in your words and actions. Do not pretend to be something you are not, changing yourself to fit every situation like a sea creature clinging to a rock. Speak truthfully and let your heart match your words.

A person who chooses to do wrong is truly evil. But if someone is forced into wrongdoing, their fate is uncertain—let each person choose what is right.

Do not be proud of your wisdom, strength, or wealth, for only God is truly wise, powerful, and rich. Do not dwell on past mistakes, as what is done cannot be undone. Control your anger, and do not act recklessly, as violence often leads to regret. Many have taken lives without meaning to, simply because they let their emotions take control.

Neither too much suffering nor too much luxury is good for people. Living in excess leads to greed and uncontrollable desires. Great wealth often leads to arrogance and cruelty. Jealousy, rage, and uncontrolled passion can drive a person to madness, leading them to act foolishly.

Righteousness is something to be proud of, while evil boldness leads to destruction. Those who are truly strong seek justice, while those who crave power bring harm. True love is good and honorable, but uncontrolled desire leads only to disgrace.

A foolish person may seem charming to others, but wisdom is found in self-control. Be moderate in eating, drinking, and conversation, for balance is the key to happiness. Too much of anything brings trouble.

Do not be envious, dishonest, or deceitful. Do not be cruel or untrustworthy. Be careful with your words and actions. Stay away from evil, and do not seek revenge—leave justice to God. Persuasion is better than conflict, for fighting only leads to more fighting. Do not trust too easily—wait to see the truth before making a decision.

This is the challenge of life, and these are the rewards. This is the path to victory and the gateway to eternal life. Those who follow it will receive honor in the eyes of God. They will pass through the gates of heaven and receive their reward.

A great sign will appear: children will be born with gray hair. People will suffer from famine, disease, and war. The times will change, and many will weep. Parents will mourn the loss of their children, burying them in the earth, which will be soaked with blood and dust.

The last generation will be full of wickedness. They will be blind to the truth, like children who refuse to understand. When women can no longer have children, it will be a sign that the end is near.

False prophets will appear, pretending to be messengers of truth. A great deceiver will rise, performing wonders to mislead the people. He will bring confusion, especially to the faithful and to the people of Israel. Many will suffer, and their belongings will be stolen. Those who hold on to their faith will face great trials, but the truth will remain.

A terrible judgment will come upon the earth. From the east, a people of twelve tribes will rise, searching for their lost Hebrew brothers and sisters who were once taken by the Assyrians. Many nations will be destroyed in this time, and these faithful and chosen Hebrews will rise to rule over others, just as they had before. Their strength will never fail.

God, who watches over all from heaven, will bring deep sleep upon many. But blessed are those who remain awake and ready when the Master returns! Those who stay watchful, never closing their eyes, will be prepared. He will come unexpectedly—at dawn, in the evening, or at midday—but he will surely come.

When that time arrives, even the stars will be visible in the middle of the day, shining alongside the sun and moon as the final moment draws near. The prophet Elijah will descend from the heavens in his celestial chariot and show the world three terrible signs that warn of destruction.

It will be a dreadful time for pregnant women and mothers caring for newborns. Those living on the seas will face disaster. A thick, dark mist will cover the entire world, blocking out the sky in every direction. Then, a river of fire will pour down from heaven, consuming everything—land, oceans, rivers, lakes, and even the depths of the underworld. The sky itself will break apart, and the stars will fall into the seas.

People will cry out in agony as they are burned by fire and sulfur. The entire world will be reduced to ashes. Every part of creation—earth, sea, sky, light, and time itself—will be gone. No birds will fly in the sky, no creatures will swim in the sea, and no ships will sail. The land will be silent—no cattle plowing fields, no winds blowing through the air. Everything will be melted down, and only what is pure will be saved.

Then, the eternal angels of God—Arakiel, Ramiel, Uriel, Samiel, and Azael—who know every wrong deed committed by mankind, will bring all souls out of the darkness and lead them to the final judgment.

The only one who is truly eternal—the almighty God—will sit as the judge of all people. Those who have died will be restored. He will give them life again, returning their souls, voices, and bodies. Bones will be rejoined, flesh will be restored, veins and skin will be remade, and hair will grow again. They will rise as living beings once more, breathing as they did before.

Then, the great angel Uriel will break open the unbreakable gates of the underworld, tearing apart the chains of darkness. He will lead out all who have suffered in the past—the ancient Titans, the mighty giants, those who drowned in the flood, those swallowed by the sea, and those devoured by beasts and birds. Every soul, no matter how they perished, will be gathered before God's judgment.

Even those who were consumed by fire will be restored and brought before the throne of judgment. The Lord of Heaven, the one who commands the thunder, will bring an end to fate itself. He will raise the dead, sit upon his heavenly throne, and establish a mighty pillar that will never fall.

Then, Christ, who can never be corrupted, will appear among the clouds, ready to bring justice to all.

Christ will come in glory with pure angels and sit at the right hand of God on the great judgment seat. He will judge both the righteous and the wicked. Moses, the great friend of God, will return in the flesh, along with Abraham, Isaac, Jacob, Joshua, Daniel, Elijah, Habakkuk, Jonah, and those who were killed by the Hebrews.

But after the prophet Jeremiah, the Hebrews who rejected the truth will face judgment. Each person will receive the punishment or reward they deserve for what they did in life.

Everyone will pass through a river of unquenchable fire. The righteous will be saved, but the wicked will be destroyed forever. Those who committed evil—murderers, liars, thieves, homewreckers, deceivers, and betrayers—will be punished. Those who worshiped idols and abandoned the true God, those who harmed the faithful and killed the righteous, and those who pretended to be holy leaders while acting unjustly will all face judgment.

People who used their power to oppress others, those who took advantage of orphans and widows, and those who grew rich through corruption will suffer for their greed. Those who refused to care for their aging parents, broke their promises, disrespected their families, or mistreated their servants will not escape punishment.

All who abused their bodies, engaged in secret sin, encouraged abortions, or abandoned their own children will face the wrath of God. Sorcerers and those who practiced magic will be judged as well. They will be bound to a pillar surrounded by a restless fire.

God's mighty angels will chain them in burning flames and strike them with terrible punishments. They will be thrown into Gehenna, a place of endless night, where monstrous beasts roam in the darkness.

The suffering of these wicked souls will be great. A fiery wheel will circle around them as they cry out in despair. Fathers, mothers, children, and even infants will wail in agony. Their suffering will be three times worse than the evil they committed.

They will be tortured by unbearable hunger and thirst, grinding their teeth in pain. They will beg for death, but it will never come. Neither night nor rest will ease their torment. They will cry out to God, but he will turn away from them.

God had given them many chances to repent, even showing them signs through a pure virgin. But they refused to listen.

However, those who lived with kindness, justice, and faith will be led by angels through the river of fire into a place of peace. There, they will find eternal life in the presence of God.

They will come to a land where three pure streams flow—one of honey, one of wine, and one of milk. The land will be shared by all, with no fences or barriers. Food will grow freely, and no one will lack anything. There will be no more rich or poor—everyone will live together in harmony.

In that time, there will be no more rulers or servants, no rich or poor, and no kings or leaders. Everyone will be equal. No one will say, "It is night," or "Tomorrow is coming," or "Yesterday has passed." There will be no more seasons—no spring, summer, fall, or winter. There will be no more marriages, deaths, buying, or selling. The sun will no longer rise or set because God will create one endless day.

For those who have lived righteously, God will grant another gift. When they ask him for mercy, he will listen. He will rescue people from the fire and suffering, saving them from endless pain. For the sake of his faithful followers, he will remove them from their torment and bring them to an everlasting life among the immortals. They will live in the beautiful fields of paradise, near the peaceful waters of an eternal lake.

But what will become of me? I was a sinner. I wasted my life chasing meaningless things, ignoring what truly mattered. I did not honor marriage or use wisdom. Even though I lived in a wealthy home, I turned away those in need. I knowingly did what was wrong.

Yet, Lord, even though I was shameless, I beg you to save me from my suffering. I ask you to show me mercy. Let me rest now from my words, Holy One, giver of all things, King of the eternal kingdom.

Book 3.

O powerful God, who rules from the heavens and commands all things, you have placed your angels where they belong. I have spoken the truth as you instructed, but now I ask for rest because my heart is weary.

Yet, why do I still feel this urge inside me? It's as if something is pushing me forward, forcing me to speak again. I cannot remain silent—I must share what God has revealed.

People of the earth, made in God's image, why do you stray so far from the right path? Why have you forgotten the one who created you? There is only one true God, the ruler of everything, beyond human understanding. No hands have ever made him, and no artist can capture his image in gold or stone.

He alone has existed forever and always will. Who among people can look upon him with their own eyes? Who can even bear to speak his holy name? With just his word, he created everything—the skies, the seas, the shining sun, the glowing moon, and the stars that fill the night. He formed the rivers, the springs, and even the eternal fire. He set the cycle of day and night in motion.

This same God made Adam, the first human, and spread his people across the world. He created the pattern of human life and all the creatures that roam the earth, swim in the seas, and fly through the sky.

Yet, instead of honoring him, people worship false gods. They bow to snakes, make offerings to cats, and pray to idols made of stone. They sit outside temples built for gods that cannot see, hear, or move, forgetting the true Creator of all things. They foolishly believe they must protect the very God who watches over them. They place their faith in lifeless statues while ignoring the judgment of the eternal Savior who made the heavens and the earth.

What a corrupt and deceitful generation! They love violence, trickery, and lies. They have no morals, committing adultery and chasing after false gods. Greed controls them, and they take whatever they desire without guilt. The rich refuse to help the poor, and wickedness spreads like a disease.

Many women will betray their husbands, seeking love elsewhere. Marriage will lose its meaning, and faithfulness will fade away.

But when Rome gains full control over Egypt and rules over all, the eternal God will establish his greatest kingdom. A holy ruler will come to govern every nation, and his kingdom will never end.

Then, destruction will fall upon the Romans. Three great disasters will strike them, bringing chaos and ruin. Many will perish as fire rains down from the heavens, burning their homes and cities.

How terrible that day will be! When will the final judgment arrive? When will the mighty God, the King of all, bring justice to the world?

For now, cities stand tall, filled with temples, markets, grand statues, and places of entertainment where people gather. But all of this is leading them toward their downfall. A time is coming when the air will reek of burning sulfur, and people in every city will suffer greatly.

I must continue to warn all nations of the troubles that are to come.

A ruler named Beliar will rise from the Sebastenes. He will reshape the land, lifting mountains and stopping the sea. The sun and moon will seem frozen in the sky, and he will even bring the dead back to life. He will perform amazing miracles in front of the people, but his power will be built on lies. Many will believe in him, including both faithful Hebrews and those who have ignored God's teachings.

But when God's judgment comes, a massive fire will fall from the sky like a great wave crashing down. It will destroy Beliar and all who trusted in him. After this, a woman will take control of the world, and everyone will obey her rule.

This widow, now the ruler of all nations, will throw gold, silver, bronze, and iron into the sea, getting rid of the riches of mortal men. Then, the world's natural order will begin to break apart. God, who rules from heaven, will roll up the sky like a scroll, and everything in the universe will collapse.

An endless fire will pour down, burning everything—the land, the oceans, the sky, and even time itself. There will be no more day or night, no more seasons—spring, summer, fall, and winter will cease to exist.

In the middle of this final age, God's judgment will take place, bringing an end to all things.

Every land and sea, from the East to the West, will bow before the one who returns. He will take control of everything, fully revealing his divine power.

Long ago, when the people of Assyria built a great tower, God warned them of his authority. They all spoke the same language and worked together to build a tower that would reach the heavens. But God sent a powerful wind that knocked it down. He scattered the people across the world and gave them different languages. From that moment, the city became known as Babylon.

After the tower fell, people spread across the earth, creating new nations and kingdoms. The tenth generation of humans was born after the great flood. During this time, Cronos, Titan, and Iapetus became rulers. People believed they were children of the earth and sky, calling them the first kings.

The world was divided into three regions, and each ruler governed his own land in peace. They swore an oath never to fight each other, and for a time, there was balance. But when their father died of old age, the brothers broke their promises. Greed and ambition led to war, and Cronos and Titan fought for control.

The goddesses Rhea, Gaia, Aphrodite, Demeter, Hestia, and Dione stepped in and convinced the rulers to end their conflict. They agreed that Cronos, as the eldest and strongest, should rule over all.

However, Titan forced Cronos to swear that he would never have a son, ensuring that Titan would inherit the throne when Cronos grew old. To make sure this happened, the Titans watched Rhea closely whenever she gave birth. They killed every baby boy and only allowed daughters to live.

But when Rhea became pregnant for the third time, she first gave birth to a daughter, Hera. The Titans, seeing a female child, believed there was no danger and left. However, soon after, Rhea secretly gave birth to a son. She made three Cretan men swear to keep her secret and sent the baby to Phrygia, where he was hidden and raised in secret. This child was Zeus, whose name meant "sent away."

Later, Rhea protected another son, Poseidon, in the same way. Finally, she gave birth to Pluto, her third son, in Dodona. Near this place, the river Europus flowed, joining with the Peneus before emptying into the sea. The waters there became known as the Stygian River, famous for its deep and mysterious nature.

When the Titans discovered that Cronos and Rhea had secretly kept their sons alive, they gathered sixty of their strongest men. They captured Cronos and Rhea, locked them in chains, and buried them deep within the earth, keeping them under guard.

But when Cronos' sons learned what had happened, they started a great war, filling the world with chaos and destruction. This was the first war among mortals, marking the beginning of endless conflicts. God punished the Titans for their deeds, and all of them, along with the children of Cronos, perished.

As time passed, new kingdoms rose. First came the Egyptian empire, followed by the Persians, the Medes, the Ethiopians, Assyrians, and Babylonians. Then, the Macedonians gained power, later followed by another period of Egyptian rule, and finally, Rome.

Then, God placed a message in my heart, instructing me to speak of what is to come. He revealed the future of nations and their rulers.

First, the kingdom of Solomon will expand, bringing together warriors from Phoenicia, Syria, the islands, Pamphylia, Persia, Phrygia, Caria, Mysia, and Lydia, a land rich in gold.

Then, the Greeks will rise—a proud and corrupt people. After them, the Macedonians will take power, a mighty and cunning nation, sweeping across the world like a great storm of war. But God will eventually destroy them completely.

Next, a great kingdom will emerge from the western sea. This empire, strong and many-headed, will conquer vast lands and strike fear into kings. They will plunder cities and steal their treasures of gold and silver. But in time, wealth will return to the earth, and luxury will rise again.

However, these rulers will become corrupt, oppressing the people. When they give in to their arrogance and greed, their downfall will begin. Wickedness will take over, and men will turn against nature itself—men will be with men, and children will be forced into disgraceful acts.

In those days, suffering will spread everywhere. Evil will disrupt life, shattering peace and bringing destruction to all. Greed and corruption will fuel endless violence, especially in Macedonia, where deceit and hatred will grow strong.

This wickedness will continue until the seventh kingdom, when an Egyptian ruler, descended from the Greeks, will take power. But then, the people of the one true God will rise again. They will become leaders and guides, teaching others how to live righteously.

God has shown me the order of things—what will come first, what will follow, and what terrible events will mark the final days. The first to face punishment will be the Titans, for they must pay for imprisoning Cronos and his beloved wife.

After them, Greece will fall under the rule of cruel and immoral kings. These rulers will be corrupt and filled with desire, bringing endless war and suffering.

The Phrygians will be wiped out, and Troy will meet disaster. The Persians and Assyrians will face ruin, as will the people of Egypt, Libya, and Ethiopia. Trouble will spread to the Carians and Pamphylians, moving from one nation to the next, bringing hardship to all of humanity.

Why list each one separately? When the first signs come true, the rest will follow quickly. Now, I will reveal the first event that will mark the beginning of these times.

There will be great suffering for the righteous people who live near Solomon's temple—those who are descendants of just and faithful men. I will tell you their origins, their families, and their land so that you may understand.

There is a city on earth called Ur of the Chaldees. From this place comes a people known for their goodness and commitment to justice. They have always valued kindness and honorable deeds above all else.

They do not waste time studying the paths of the sun and moon or searching for signs in the depths of the ocean. They do not believe in fortune tellers, enchanters, or those who claim to see the future through meaningless tricks.

Unlike the Chaldeans, they do not rely on astrology or the stars to guide their lives. These practices only mislead people, keeping them trapped in endless searching while failing to teach them anything truly valuable.

Lies and deception led many people away from the right path, filling the world with evil. These false teachings turned people away from truth and justice. But those who live righteously reject greed, knowing that it leads to war, famine, and endless suffering. They live honestly, treating others fairly, both in cities and in the countryside. They do not steal or take what does not belong to them. They do not move land markers to claim another person's property. The wealthy do not oppress the poor or cause widows to suffer. Instead, they help those in need, sharing their wheat, wine, and oil.

Those who have more always give a portion of their harvest to those who have little, following God's law. He created the earth to be shared by all.

When the twelve tribes of Israel leave Egypt, guided by God, they will travel at night under a pillar of fire and by day with a cloud leading their way. God will choose Moses to lead them. A princess will find him as a baby near a marsh, take him in, and raise him as her own child. When he grows up, God will use him to guide his people out of Egypt to Mount Sinai.

On that mountain, God will give them his laws. He will write his commandments on two stone tablets, teaching them how to live righteously. Anyone who disobeys these laws will face punishment, either from people or from God himself. No one will escape judgment.

For seventy years, their land and temple will be left in ruins. But in the end, they will be restored and honored, just as God has promised. They must remain faithful and trust in his laws. One day, he will lift them out of their suffering and bring them back into the light.

Then, God will send a king from heaven to judge all people with fire and blood. A royal family will continue to rule, and over time, they will rebuild God's temple. The Persian kings will provide the materials—bronze, gold, and iron—because God will send them visions in their dreams. The temple will be restored to its former glory.

After I spoke these words, I prayed to God for rest. But once again, he placed a message in my heart, commanding me to share it with the world, even with the rulers of nations.

God revealed to me the suffering that would come upon Babylon for destroying his temple.

Babylon, your time of destruction is near! The earth will shake as violence spreads. The cries of destruction will rise, and God's hand will strike down your land. From above, disaster will fall upon you as punishment from heaven.

Your children will be wiped out, their souls taken by the Eternal One. It will be as if you had never existed. But your land will be filled with blood, just as you once shed the blood of good and righteous people. Their cries still reach the heavens.

Egypt, you too will suffer. You believed you were safe, but disaster will strike. A sword will pass through your cities, bringing death, famine, and ruin. This suffering will last through seven generations of kings before it ends.

Land of Gog and Magog, near the rivers of Ethiopia, your streets will be covered in blood. Your land will become a place of judgment, filled with death and destruction.

Libya, your suffering is coming as well. The western lands and the sea itself will face a dark day. War will chase you down, bringing violence and destruction.

You destroyed the house of the Immortal God, tearing it apart with iron. Because of this, your land will be covered with the dead—killed by war, famine, disease, and enemy attacks. Your cities will be abandoned, left in ruins.

In the West, a bright star will appear in the sky, a comet bringing a warning. It will be a sign of war, famine, death, and the downfall of kings and rulers.

Strange signs will appear everywhere. The Tanais River will break away from Lake Maeotis, and new land will rise where there was once only water. Rivers will change their course, and deep cracks will open in the earth, swallowing entire cities.

Many places will be destroyed, including cities in Asia—like Iassus, Cebren, Pandonia, Colophon, Ephesus, Nicaea, Antioch, Sinope, Smyrna, Myrina, and Gaza. In Europe, places like Tanagra, Clitor, Basilis, Meropeia, Antigone, Magnesia, Mycenae, and Oiantheia will also fall.

Egypt's power will soon come to an end. The past will be better than the future for the people of Alexandria.

Rome will be repaid for its actions. The riches it once took from Asia will be returned threefold. The destruction it caused will be repaid with its own suffering.

Just as many people from Asia were once taken as servants in Rome, even more Romans will become slaves in Asia. They will be trapped in poverty, buried in debt, and stripped of their wealth.

Rome, you were once proud, celebrating in luxury, drinking at grand feasts. But now, you will be a slave, forced into shameful marriages. The women of Rome will be humiliated, their beauty taken away. They will be dishonored, their hair cut, their dignity lost.

The rulers of the land will be overthrown, and no one will show them mercy. Corrupt leaders will destroy the people, using their power for evil instead of justice.

Samos will turn to dust, Delos will lose its brightness, and Rome will become nothing but an empty space. But everything God has planned will happen exactly as he said. Peace will come to the lands of Asia, and Europe will finally know happiness. The land will be full of life, free from storms and disasters. The air will be clean, and the fields will be filled with food. Animals, birds, and all living things will flourish.

People will live in joy, their homes filled with happiness. From the heavens, justice and order will guide humanity. People will treat each other with kindness and trust, welcoming strangers with open hearts. Evil will disappear—greed, jealousy, anger, and foolishness will be gone. There will be no more poverty, violence, war, or crime.

But Macedonia will bring pain to Asia, and Europe will suffer from a corrupt and undeserving family. Born from both rulers and slaves, they will conquer Babylon and claim to rule all the lands under the sun. But in time, they will fall, and their name will only be remembered far into the future.

Then, a man unlike any before will rise in Asia. He will wear a purple robe, be ruthless and unfair, and crave power. The god of thunder will push him forward. Under his rule, Asia will suffer, its lands soaked in blood. But the underworld will take him away, and the very people he tried to destroy will wipe out his family.

Out of this chaos, a new leader will rise. He will cut down a powerful ruler and take his place. A son will kill his own father, a great warrior, and the god of war himself will fall at the hands of his grandson. Soon after, the new ruler will take control, replacing the old one.

In Phrygia, a terrible sign will appear. When the cursed descendants of Rhea suddenly vanish overnight—along with an entire city—it will be a warning of disaster. The god of the sea, Poseidon, will shake the land, tearing down walls and breaking the earth open. The city of Dorylaeum in Phrygia will be destroyed, and the world will forever remember this as the time of the "Earth-shaker."

But this event will not bring peace—it will mark the beginning of great suffering. A terrible war will spread across the land. The descendants of Aeneas, born from the bloodline of Ilus, will bring destruction, and their city will eventually fall to greedy invaders.

Troy, your fate is sealed. In Sparta, a beautiful and powerful woman will rise, and her actions will send waves of destruction across Asia and Europe. But you, Troy, will suffer the most. Endless war, pain, and sorrow will follow, yet your name will live on in history.

During this time, an old man will appear. He will call himself a writer, though no one will know where he truly comes from. His eyesight will fail, but his mind will stay sharp, and his poetry will be admired. He will claim to be from Chios and write about Troy, but his words will not be entirely true—only beautifully written.

This man will use my words, opening my writings for the first time. But he will change them, turning them into grand tales of warriors in shining armor. He will make Hector, son of Priam, and Achilles, son of Peleus, into legendary figures of war. He will add gods to their battles, creating false stories. His version of history will make the deaths of these warriors seem noble. But in return, he will receive great praise for his work.

A group from Lycia will bring suffering to the people of Locri. Chalcedon, which guards a narrow sea passage, will one day be attacked by a young warrior from Aetolia. The wealthy city of Cyzicus will be shattered by the sea. Byzantium, the city of Ares, will be destroyed by an army from Asia, drowning in blood and sorrow.

The great mountain Cragus in Lycia will shake, causing deep cracks to form. Water will rush from the broken rock, and the oracles of Patara will fall silent forever. Cyzicus, near the wine-rich Propontis, will be hit by the raging waves of the Rhyndacus River.

Rhodes, island of the sun, you will enjoy many years of freedom and success. You will rule the seas and grow strong. But in time, greedy men will take over, weighing you down with heavy burdens because of your beauty and wealth.

A massive earthquake will strike Lydia, shaking Persia and causing terrible destruction. The people of Europe and Asia will suffer greatly.

A cruel king from Sidon will bring destruction to the seafaring people of Samos. Blood will flow through the land and mix with the sea. The noble women and brides will cry in sorrow, grieving for their husbands and sons who have been lost.

Cyprus, a powerful earthquake will shake your land, taking many lives. The underworld will claim the souls of those who die together.

Trallis, near Ephesus, despite your strong walls and great wealth, you will also fall to an earthquake. The ground will split open, releasing boiling water from deep below, and the earth will tremble with unstoppable force.

Flames and the choking smell of burning sulfur will destroy those who are trapped by its power. One day, Samos will build great royal palaces.

Italy, you will not be invaded by enemies from other lands, but your own people will turn against each other in violent battles. Bloodshed between your own tribes will leave you empty and broken. In the end, you will be covered in ashes, never realizing that your downfall was your own doing. You will no longer be a land of great leaders, but a place where wild beasts roam.

A merciless ruler will rise from Italy and bring destruction. Laodicea, the beautiful city of the Carians by the Lycus River, you will fall, mourning in silence for the ancestors you once honored.

The Thracian Crobyzi will rise from the Haemus Mountains. The people of Campania will suffer, grinding their teeth in despair as famine devours them. Corsica will grieve the loss of its elders, and Sardinia will sink beneath the sea under the force of powerful storms and divine punishment. Those who live by the sea will look on in shock at this great disaster.

So many young women will die. Countless young men will drown in the deep, their bodies lost without a proper burial. Helpless children will perish, and great treasures will be swallowed by the sea.

Mysia will see a royal family rise to power. Chalcedon will soon come to an end. Galatia will suffer greatly, and Tenedos will face its final and most terrible disaster. Sicyon and Corinth will cry out in sorrow, yet they will still boast, as flutes play their mournful songs.

When my soul had a moment of rest, God placed another message in my heart. He commanded me to reveal what is yet to come.

A terrible fate awaits the people of Phoenicia—the men, the women, and all the cities by the sea. Not one of you will survive to see the sunlight, for your time is coming to an end. Your people will vanish because of your lies and wicked ways. You spoke false words, lived without honor, and turned your backs on God, the true King.

Because of this, destruction will come upon you. A great fire will rise from the earth, consuming your cities until only ruins remain where mighty buildings once stood.

Crete, a disaster is coming. A devastating blow will strike, and the

Almighty will bring great destruction. Smoke will rise, covering the sky. The flames will not die out, and your land will burn until nothing is left.

Thrace, your people will be enslaved. The Galatians will join forces with the sons of Dardanus, invading Greece and bringing devastation. Your land will be taken from you, and you will give away much but receive nothing in return.

Gog, Magog, and all the people of Mardia and Daia—great suffering is waiting for you.

Lycia, Mysia, and Phrygia will also feel the weight of this disaster. Many people from Pamphylia, Lydia, Caria, Cappadocia, Ethiopia, and Arabia will fall. There are too many to name, but every nation will be struck by the plague that the Almighty will send.

A brutal army will invade Greece. They will kill strong leaders and slaughter countless sheep, horses, mules, and cattle. They will burn down homes, leaving nothing behind. They will take many prisoners— men, women, and children—forcing them into slavery. Young brides will be torn from their homes, their feet barely touching the ground as they are dragged away. Their captors, speaking a language they do not understand, will bind them in chains and treat them cruelly.

No one will come to save them. They will watch as their enemies take everything—their wealth, their homes, their lands. Their legs will tremble in fear.

A hundred men will flee, but one enemy will chase them all down. Five soldiers will be enough to scatter an entire army. The people will turn against one another in shameful battles, bringing joy to their enemies but suffering upon themselves.

Then, all of Greece will be enslaved. War and disease will come together, bringing suffering to everyone. God will turn the sky into hard bronze and the earth into iron. No rain will fall, and drought will cover the land. Crops will wither, and the ground will crack under the burning heat.

People will cry out in pain and hunger, but there will be no relief. The Creator of heaven and earth will send fire down, and only one-third of mankind will survive.

Greece, why do you put your trust in leaders who are only human and cannot escape death? Why do you make foolish offerings to idols? Who convinced you to follow this false path and turn away from the one true God?

Remember the Almighty and do not forget his name. It has been 1,500 years since proud rulers first led Greece. They introduced false gods to the people, creating statues for worship and filling hearts with foolish beliefs.

But when the wrath of the Almighty comes, you will finally see the truth. People will lift their hands to the sky in despair, crying out for help. They will beg for a savior to rescue them from the great disaster that is coming.

Listen and remember these words in your hearts, for hard times will come in the years ahead.

If Greece offers sacrifices of bulls and cows to the great God, she will escape from war, fear, and deadly sickness. She will break free from oppression. But until that time, there will still be people who turn away from God, even when the final day arrives.

You must not make offerings to God until everything he has planned is completed. Nothing he has decided will fail to happen, and events will unfold with great force.

One day, there will be a new generation of faithful people who follow God's teachings and live by his wisdom. They will honor his temple with offerings, burnt sacrifices, and gifts of bulls, rams, lambs, and the best of their flocks. They will offer these sacrifices with pure hearts on God's great altar.

Living by his laws, they will be blessed, and their cities and fields will be full of riches. God will send prophets to guide them, bringing great joy to all people. Only they will receive his wisdom and have faith and righteous hearts.

They will not be misled by worthless things or worship idols made of gold, bronze, silver, or stone. They will not bow to statues or lifeless images created by human hands. Instead, they will raise their hands to heaven in prayer, waking early each morning to cleanse themselves with water and honor the eternal God.

They will respect their parents and remain faithful to their marriages. They will not engage in disgraceful acts like the Phoenicians, Latins, Egyptians, Greeks, Persians, Galatians, and many others who have broken God's laws. Because these nations have disobeyed him, they will suffer. God will send famine, pain, war, disease, and sorrow upon them for refusing to worship him.

Instead of honoring the one true God, people will worship man-made idols. But when a young king—Egypt's seventh ruler since the Greeks took control—comes to power, they will realize their mistakes.

A great ruler from Asia will come like a fiery eagle, bringing his army on foot and horseback. He will spread destruction across the land, fill it with suffering, and overthrow Egypt. He will take away its wealth, carrying it across the sea.

Then, before the eternal King, people will kneel in submission, bowing on the earth that has long provided for them. All the idols they made with their own hands will be destroyed by fire.

At last, God will bless the people. The land will flourish, and trees and flocks will provide in abundance. Wine, honey, milk, and wheat—the best gifts for humankind—will be plentiful.

But you, who live with clever tricks and deceit, do not waste time. Stop hesitating and turn back to God. Offer sacrifices of bulls, lambs, and goats as the seasons change. Seek his mercy, for he is the only true God—there is no other.

Live with justice and do not oppress others. This is what the Almighty commands of all people.

Pay attention, for the wrath of God will be great. A terrible plague will sweep across the earth, and people will face harsh judgment. Kings will rise against kings, stealing lands and waging war. Nations will destroy each other, and rulers will rob entire tribes of their homes and riches.

Leaders will flee to other lands, and new rulers will take control. Foreign powers will invade Greece, taking its wealth and leaving the land in ruins. The people will turn against each other, fighting over gold and silver. Greed will lead their cities like a heartless ruler.

Many will die without a proper burial, their bodies left for vultures and wild animals. The earth will be covered in their remains, left unplowed and abandoned for years. The land will show the shame of those who turned away from what is right, with scattered weapons and broken shields. Even the forests will be untouched, as no one will cut wood for fire.

Then, God will send a king from the East to bring peace to the world. He will put an end to war, killing some enemies and forcing others to swear oaths of loyalty. But he will not act on his own, instead following the commands of the Almighty.

Under his rule, the temple of God will be restored, filled with treasures of gold, silver, and fine cloth. The land and sea will once again overflow with abundance.

But jealousy will turn kings against one another, leading them to fight and destroy themselves. In their greed, they will seek to plunder God's temple and harm the most righteous people. When they arrive in the land, wicked rulers will place their thrones around the holy city, bringing people who do not follow God's ways.

Then, the Almighty will speak with a mighty voice, calling out to those who are foolish and arrogant. His judgment will come upon them, and they will be destroyed by his power.

Flaming swords will fall from the sky, and bright lights will blaze down upon the earth. The land will shake, and the creatures of the sea and land, along with all people, will tremble before the Immortal One. Fear will spread everywhere.

Towering mountains will crack apart, and great hills will crumble. Deep chasms will open, revealing the dark underworld. Valleys will be filled with the dead, and rivers will run red with blood, spilling into the plains.

The strongholds of the wicked will collapse because they ignored the laws and judgment of the Almighty. With reckless hearts, they attacked the temple, raising their weapons against it. But God will judge them with war, fire, storms, and destruction. Fiery hail, sulfur, and great stones will rain from the sky, and even the animals will suffer.

Then, they will finally recognize the true God. But it will be too late. Cries of terror will rise from the earth as countless people perish. The wicked will be drenched in blood, and the land itself will drink deeply of the fallen. Wild beasts will feast on the dead.

All these things have been revealed to me by the eternal God, and they will surely come to pass. Everything he has placed in my heart is true, for his spirit never lies.

But the children of God will return to live in peace around the temple. They will rejoice in the blessings given by their Creator, the just Judge and mighty King. He will be their protector, surrounding them like a wall of fire. They will live in their cities and land without fear of war, for they will no longer need weapons to defend themselves.

There will be no more battles, for the Almighty himself will guard them and keep them safe.

Then everyone will see how much God loves those who stay faithful to him. Even the sun, moon, and sky will help them in their struggles and lead them to victory.

In that time, people will sing songs of praise:

"Let us fall to the ground and pray to the eternal King, the one true God. Let us go to his temple together, for he alone is Lord. Let us follow the laws of the Most High, for they are the most just on earth. We have wandered far from his path, foolishly worshiping idols made by human hands, statues of dead men."

The hearts of the faithful will be moved, and they will cry out:

"Come, let us bow before God's house and sing to him with joy. Our land has been freed from enemies, and for seven generations, we will be surrounded by their abandoned weapons—shields, helmets, bows, and arrows. No one will need to cut wood for fire, for we will have all we need."

But Greece, you must let go of your pride and seek wisdom. Turn to the Almighty with humility, for he is merciful but also just.

Do not stir up conflict with those who come from God's holy land.

Do not try to move what should remain still, or awaken a beast from its den, or invite disaster upon yourself. Let go of your arrogance and seek peace. Serve the Almighty so that you may share in his blessings.

When the final day comes, and God's judgment arrives, the earth will produce endless fruit—wheat, wine, and oil in abundance. Sweet honey will pour from the heavens, and trees will be heavy with fruit. Sheep and cattle will multiply, and the fields will be rich with crops. Rivers of milk will flow freely, bringing nourishment to all.

There will be no more war, no more suffering. The earth will no longer shake in fear. Drought, famine, and storms will disappear. A great and lasting peace will cover the world. Kings will no longer fight but will live as friends until the end of time.

God, who rules over the stars, will bring justice to all people, judging their actions. He alone is God, and there is no other. He will put an end to human cruelty, burning away evil with fire.

So change your ways. Turn away from false worship. Serve the one true God. Stay away from adultery and wickedness. Raise your children and do not take innocent lives, for God is angered by those who commit such sins.

Then, God will establish a kingdom that will last forever. He will fulfill his promises to the faithful, opening every land and blessing them with eternal joy. People from every nation will bring offerings of incense and gifts to his temple, for there will be no other place of worship—only the one God has chosen for his people.

In those days, travel will be safe. Roads through valleys, mountains, and even across the sea will be easy to cross. Peace will cover the land. Prophets of God will remove all weapons, for they will be the true leaders and just rulers of the people. There will be no more greed, only fairness and righteousness, for this is God's will.

Rejoice, for the Creator of heaven and earth has given you joy. He will dwell among you, and all life will live in harmony. Wolves and lambs will graze together. Leopards will rest beside baby goats. Bears and cattle will share the same pastures. Lions will eat straw like oxen, and little children will lead them without fear.

Deadly snakes and scorpions will no longer be a danger. Infants will sleep beside them, unharmed, for God's hand will protect them all.

Now, I give you this clear sign so that you will know when the end of all things is near.

When the end comes, there will be signs in the sky. At night, swords of light will stretch across the heavens, pointing both east and west. A thick cloud of dust will rise and spread across the earth.

The sun will darken in the middle of the sky, and the moon's light will disappear and then return again. Blood will drip from the rocks as a warning, and in the clouds, people will see visions of armies—soldiers on foot and horseback, moving like hunters chasing wild animals through heavy fog.

This will be the final moment, the time when God, who rules from the heavens, brings everything to an end. But before that happens, all people must turn to him and offer their devotion to the one true King.

I tell you these things because I left the great city of Babylon behind to warn the people of Greece about God's coming wrath. Fire will be sent down from above as punishment.

I was given the gift of prophecy to reveal divine mysteries to mortals. Some will say that I come from a faraway land, that I was born in Erythrae, and call me a liar. Others will claim I am a Sibyl, the daughter of Circe and Gnostos, mad and deceitful. But when these events come to pass, you will remember my words. No one will doubt that I was a prophet of the great God.

He showed me what happened to those who came before us and revealed the first moments of creation. He placed knowledge in my heart so that I could speak of the future and remind people of the past.

Long ago, when the earth was covered in a great flood, only one righteous man was saved. He and his family, along with animals of every kind, sailed in a wooden ark so that life could begin again.

I was married to his son and came from his bloodline. Because of this, I have seen both the first and the last of all things, and I have spoken the truth as it was revealed to me.

Book 4.

People of Asia and Europe, listen carefully to my words. I speak the truth, not as a false prophet of Apollo, whom foolish men call a god, but as a messenger of the one true God. He is not a lifeless statue made by human hands, nor is he confined to a temple built of stone.

No one can see or measure him, for he is beyond human sight. He rules over both night and day, the sun, moon, and stars, the land, the seas, the rivers, and all living creatures. He controls the rain, which brings fruit to the trees, grain to the fields, and oil from the earth.

God has placed this message in my heart, urging me to tell people what has happened and what will come, from the first generation to the eleventh. Everything I say will be proven true by the events that unfold. Listen carefully to the Sibyl, who speaks only what is right.

Blessed are those who love and honor the mighty God. They should praise him before they eat or drink and live with faith. They must not worship false idols, lifeless statues made of stone. Those who choose to live in wickedness will mock the righteous, accusing them of wrongdoing while they themselves commit evil.

People are slow to believe the truth, but when the day of judgment comes, when God separates the righteous from the wicked, then they will understand. The sinful will be cast into darkness, while the faithful will remain on the earth, blessed with life and grace.

This will happen in the tenth generation. But first, I will tell of the events from the beginning.

The Assyrians will be the first to rule over mankind, holding power for six generations after God, in his anger, covered the world with a great flood. Then the Medes will rise and take control, but they will rule for only two generations.

During this time, the world will see terrifying signs. At midday, darkness will cover the sky, and the sun, moon, and stars will vanish. A great earthquake will shake the land, destroying many cities. Even the islands of the sea will be revealed as the waters shift.

When the Euphrates River turns red with blood, a great war will break out between the Medes and the Persians. The Medes will suffer a crushing defeat, forced to flee beyond the Tigris River. The Persians will then rise to power, becoming the strongest nation in the world for a generation.

But their rule will bring chaos. War, murder, rebellion, and destruction will spread. Towers will crumble, cities will fall, and many will be exiled. Greece, in its great strength, will cross the Hellespont, bringing sorrow to Phrygia and disaster to Asia.

Egypt, the land of many fields, will suffer greatly. A terrible famine will strike, and for twenty years, the land will be barren. The Nile, the river that nourishes the crops, will no longer provide for the people.

Deep underground, dark waters will continue to flow.

A powerful king will come from Asia, leading countless ships and carrying a spear. He will travel across the sea, cutting through mountains to clear his path. After fleeing from battle, he will seek safety in Asia.

In Sicily, a fiery river will set the land on fire as Mount Etna erupts, sending flames into the sky. The great city of Croton will collapse into a deep pit.

In Greece, brutal wars will break out. Cities will be destroyed, and many lives will be lost. Both sides will suffer equally.

When the tenth generation of people arrives, Persia will fall under oppression and fear. The Macedonians will rise to power and destroy Thebes. The Carians will take over Tyre, wiping out its people.

Babylon may look strong, but it will prove weak in battle. Its high walls will not protect it as expected. Macedonians will settle in Bactria, while people from Susa and Bactria will escape to Greece.

One day, the Pyramus River will flood and reach the sacred island. When the earth shakes, cities like Cibyra and Cyzicus will fall apart. Sand will bury Samos, erasing it from sight. Delos will disappear completely. Rhodes will suffer its worst disaster yet.

The Macedonian empire will not last. A great war will come from the west, and Italy will take control. The world will be ruled by its heavy hand, and even the Italians themselves will suffer under its power.

Corinth, your downfall is coming. Carthage, your towers will crumble, and your walls will be flattened to the ground.

Laodicea, an earthquake will tear you down, turning everything to rubble. But in time, you will be rebuilt.

Lycia and Myra, the earth will never hold you steady. You will fall, and like strangers in your own land, you will beg for escape. Patara will be silenced by storms and earthquakes, punished for its wickedness.

Armenia, you will become enslaved.

War will come from Italy to Jerusalem, destroying God's great temple.

When the people of Jerusalem turn away from their faith and commit terrible crimes near the temple, a powerful ruler will rise in Italy. Like a fugitive, he will flee across the Euphrates, staying hidden from sight. He will commit terrible crimes, even killing his own mother, believing in his own cruelty.

Blood will flow in the streets of Rome as many fight for the throne. The land will be soaked in the blood of its own people.

A leader from Syria will rise in Rome. He will burn the temple in Jerusalem and massacre many Jewish people, leaving their homeland in ruins.

A massive earthquake will destroy Salamis and Paphos. Huge waves will crash over Cyprus, drowning the island.

When fire erupts from deep within Italy, shooting flames into the sky, many cities will burn, and countless lives will be lost. Thick black ash will cover the land, and red dust will rain down from the heavens.

This will be a sign of God's anger, because the people will have destroyed those who were faithful to Him.

War will break out in the West, and chaos will spread. A fugitive from Rome will rise, carrying a great spear, bringing destruction as he marches forward.

The mighty Euphrates River will be filled with countless bodies.

Oh, unfortunate Antioch, you will no longer be called a city when you fall to enemy spears because of your own mistakes.

On the island of Scyros, a deadly plague and violent battles will bring destruction.

Oh, poor Cyprus, a massive wave will rise and cover your land, tossing you into chaos as fierce storm winds whip through your shores.

Wealth will flow into Asia, the same riches that Rome once stole and stored in its grand homes. But Rome will be forced to return twice as much, and with it, war will spread even more.

The beautiful cities along the Maeander River, surrounded by tall towers, will be ruined by a terrible famine when the river hides its dark waters.

When humanity turns away from righteousness, and truth and justice disappear from the world, people will become reckless and violent. They will take pleasure in doing wrong, ignoring the good, and destroying the righteous. Their hands will be stained with blood, and they will celebrate their own cruelty like foolish children.

When this happens, know that God will no longer be patient. His fury will be unleashed, and he will destroy the human race with a great fire.

Oh, foolish mortals, change your ways before it is too late! Do not provoke the mighty God's wrath. Put away your swords and stop your violence. End the killing, the cruelty, and the senseless destruction. Wash yourselves in pure waters, raise your hands to heaven, and ask for forgiveness. If you truly repent and turn back to what is right, God will have mercy on you. He will hold back his anger and spare the world.

But if you refuse to listen and continue in your wicked ways, a great fire will cover the earth. A terrifying sign will come, with the sound of trumpets and clashing swords at sunrise. The whole world will shake from the noise. God will burn the land, destroy every city, and wipe out the rivers and seas. Everything will turn to black ash.

When everything has turned to dust and the flames have died down, God will calm the great fire he has sent. Then, from the ashes, he will rebuild the bones of men and bring them back to life, just as they were before.

At that time, he will hold the final judgment. God himself will judge the world once more. Those who lived with wicked hearts will be buried beneath the earth, never to rise again.

Book 5.

Listen carefully and remember the difficult times that will come for the people of Latium.

First, after the rulers of Egypt have fallen and been buried, and after the man from Pella who conquered both the East and West has died—his body abandoned by Babylon, proving false the claim that he was a son of Zeus—a new ruler will rise. He will come from the bloodline of Assaracus, a descendant of Troy, and he will survive the fires of destruction. After him, many leaders will take power—some will be great warriors, while others will be inexperienced and weak.

The first of these rulers will have a name connected to the number twenty. He will be strong in war. After him, another will rule, with a name that begins with the first letter of the alphabet. He will bring Thrace and Sicily under his control, and Memphis will fall because of weak rulers and a free-spirited woman who is lost at sea.

This ruler will establish laws and rule over many nations. After a long time, he will pass his power to another whose name is linked to the number three hundred and a river. This new ruler will command Persia and Babylon and will defeat the Medes in battle.

Then another ruler will come, marked by the number three. After him, a new leader will rise, his name connected to the number twenty. He will sail far across the ocean and reach the shores of Italy.

Next, a ruler with a name linked to the number fifty will appear. He will be like a fierce serpent, bringing war and destruction. But eventually, he will turn on his own people, causing chaos. He will seek fame through chariot races and great battles, leaving behind a trail of blood. He will carve a path through two seas, but in the end, he will disappear. He will return, claiming to be a god, but the true God will show his power over him.

After this, three kings will rise, only to destroy each other. Then, a cruel ruler whose name carries the number seventy will come to power. He will bring great suffering to the faithful. His son, marked by the number three hundred, will take the throne next. After him, a ruler with the number four will rise, bringing destruction.

Another leader with the number fifty in his name will come next. Then, one marked by the number three hundred will take the throne— a warrior from the Celtic lands. But he will not escape a terrible fate. After many battles, he will die on foreign land, buried in dust named after the Nemean flower.

Following him, another ruler will rise, wearing a silver helmet and carrying the name of a sea. He will be the greatest of them all, wise in his ways. His rule will bring change, and his descendants will witness these events unfold.

After him, three more rulers will take power, but the last one will rule for a long time.

I am tired, weighed down by this vision, but I must share what I have seen.

First, wild women will dance around the steps of your once-glorious temple, bringing destruction. A time will come when the Nile overflows, covering Egypt with sixteen cubits of water. It will flood the land, bringing rich soil for crops, but it will also mark a time of great change. Egypt's beauty will remain, but its power will fade.

Memphis, you will mourn more than any other city in Egypt. Once strong, you will become poor and weak. The great voice from the heavens will cry out:

"Oh, mighty Memphis, you once ruled over fearful men, but now you will suffer! You will cry out in pain and sorrow. Only then will you recognize the eternal God, the one who rules above the clouds.

Where is your pride now? You stood against my chosen people and brought suffering upon the righteous. Now you will pay the same price. You will no longer stand among the blessed."

"You have fallen from the stars and will never rise to heaven again."

God commanded me to deliver this final warning to Egypt, for the time will come when people become completely corrupt. Evil men will continue their wicked ways, but punishment awaits them—the wrath of the mighty one in heaven. Instead of worshiping God, they will bow to stones and animals. They will fear lifeless things that have no voice, no mind, and no power to hear their prayers.

It is not right for me to name these false gods, but they are nothing more than idols, created by human hands. People have made their own gods from wood, stone, bronze, gold, and silver, melting them in fire and trusting in things that cannot think or speak.

Thmois and Xois will suffer greatly, and the great temples of Heracles, Zeus, and Hermes will be struck down.

Alexandria, once a powerful city, will face endless war and disease.

Because of your pride, you will suffer the same pain you once caused. Silence will fall over you for many years, and your time of restoration will be distant. No longer will you enjoy your rich and abundant pleasures.

A Persian invader will come into your land like a storm, bringing destruction. He will fill the land with bloodshed, slaughtering many. A ruthless, mindless leader will rush into battle with countless soldiers, leaving nothing but ruin behind.

Wealthy cities will become exhausted and broken. All of Asia will weep, once adorned with riches, now stripped of everything she once loved. The conqueror who seizes Persia will bring war, wiping out almost all life. Only a third of the people will survive his wrath.

From the West, he will move swiftly, taking control of lands, destroying everything in his path. When he reaches his full power and is feared by many, he will set his sights on attacking the city of the blessed.

But God will send a mighty king against him—one who will destroy the strongest rulers and bravest warriors. This will be the moment when the immortal one brings judgment upon the world.

Oh, my sorrowful heart! Why must I speak of these painful times? Egypt's rule over many lands will bring suffering.

Turn instead to the East, to the Persians—people lacking wisdom—and warn them of what is happening now and what is still to come.

The Euphrates River will overflow, bringing destruction. The flood will wipe out the Persians, Iberians, Babylonians, and the war-loving Massagetae, who foolishly rely on their bows. Fire will spread across all of Asia, burning so brightly it will be seen from the islands.

The once-revered city of Pergamos will be completely destroyed. Pitane will become a wasteland.

All of Lesbos will sink beneath the waves, disappearing into the sea. Smyrna, once honored, will be thrown from her cliffs, crying out as she perishes completely.

The people of Bithynia will mourn over their land, reduced to ashes. Great Syria and the many tribes of Phoenicia will also fall into ruin.

Lycia, so much suffering will come upon you! The sea itself will rise against you, flooding the land and bringing disasters.

A great earthquake will strike, and bitter waters will crash onto the once-fragrant lands of Lycia, turning beauty into devastation.

Phrygia will face terrible destruction, bringing sorrow to Rhea, the mother of Zeus, who once stayed there for a long time.

The sea will rise and wipe out the Centaur race and a fierce nation, while the land of the Lapiths will be swallowed beneath the earth.

The deep and fast-flowing Peneus River will flood Thessaly, sweeping away its people. Eridanus, once known for its strange waters, will bring further disaster.

Greece will suffer terribly, and poets will mourn for her when a ruler from Italy strikes at the isthmus. This powerful Roman king, who is treated like a god, will rise to power. Some will even claim he is the son of Zeus and Hera.

This ruler, who charms people with his beautiful voice and songs, will commit great evil. He will kill many, including his own mother.

A feared and shameless leader from Babylon will flee. People will despise him because of his many crimes—he took the lives of countless people, defiled the wombs of women, and committed terrible sins against his own wives.

He will seek refuge with the kings of the Medes and Persians, the same people he once honored and helped rise to power. But alongside wicked men, he will secretly plot against an unwanted nation.

He will seize God's holy temple and attack its people. Those who entered the temple in faith will be burned. When this man appears, the whole world will tremble. Kings will fall, but his power will remain, leading to the destruction of a great city and the suffering of righteous people.

In the fourth year of these events, a great star will shine brightly, dominating the sky. It will hold special significance, tied to the honor once given to Poseidon.

Then, another massive star will fall from the heavens into the sea, setting the waters ablaze. Its fire will reach Babylon, Italy, and other lands, bringing destruction as punishment for the deaths of many faithful Hebrews and innocent people.

You, sinful city, will suffer greatly. You will be abandoned, left empty and desolate for ages. You will despise your own land, but it will be too late.

You gave yourself to sorcery, committed adultery, and indulged in shameful and unnatural acts. You were an evil, corrupt, and unjust city—more cursed than all others.

Oh, city of Latium, you are impure in every way! Like a frenzied woman who delights in snakes, you will sit alone, widowed, on the banks of the Tiber River.

The river itself will mourn for you, its once-proud partner, now filled with blood and sin.

Did you not understand the power of God and his plans? You

thought yourself untouchable, saying, "I am invincible—no one can destroy me."

But now, the eternal God will bring ruin upon you and everything you possess. Your banners will no longer wave in the land as they once did when you received honor from God.

Now you will be left alone, abandoned in a fiery prison, dwelling in the burning depths of the underworld.

And once again, I grieve for Egypt, lost in blindness.

Memphis, you will be overrun with the dead. The pyramids will echo with the cries of those who suffer.

Python, once known as the twin city, you will fall silent for generations, forced to abandon your wickedness.

A land filled with suffering and pain, a place of endless sorrow—you will be left as a weeping widow. You ruled the world for many years, but your time is over.

When the unclean land is covered by the white robes of purity, I will wish I had never been born to witness it.

Thebes, where is your great strength now? A fierce man will slaughter your people. You will be left alone, dressed in mourning, crying out in despair.

You will be punished for the sins of your past. Those who remain will see the price of lawlessness and evil.

A mighty leader from Ethiopia will rise and overthrow Syene, showing the power of his people.

Dark-skinned warriors from India will take over Teucheira.

Pentapolis, a mighty leader will burn your cities to the ground. Libya, full of sorrow, who will explain your mistakes? And Cyrene, who will mourn for you? Even in your final moments, your cries will not stop.

Across Britain and Gaul, where gold is plentiful, the ocean will roar with the sound of battle, stained red with blood. These lands brought suffering upon God's people when a king of the Sidonians, a Phoenician leader, led a great army of Gauls from Syria.

This army will bring destruction upon you, Ravenna, leading you to slaughter.

People of India and Ethiopia, beware. When Capricorn and Taurus align in the sky, with Virgo rising, the sun will lead the heavens in a new direction. A massive fire will descend from the sky, reshaping the stars in battle, and Ethiopia will be consumed by flames, drowning in sorrow.

Corinth, prepare to weep for your own destruction. When the three sisters of fate spin their threads, they will guide a deceiver to power. He will stand before the isthmus, where a man once carved through rock with metal tools. This leader will bring ruin to your land, as fate has decided.

God will grant him the power to do what no other ruler before him could achieve. He will first cut down three great leaders, feeding their remains to others. Unholy kings will feast upon the flesh of their own families. Death and terror will spread across the land because of a great city and a righteous people who were preserved by divine will.

Oh, foolish and reckless one, surrounded by disaster! You bring both suffering and the promise of restoration to the world. A leader full of arrogance, a curse upon humanity—who ever wished for you? Who has not suffered because of you?

A mighty king will fall because of you, losing his honorable life.

You have turned everything upside down, destroying all that was once beautiful. You have changed the world's order, bringing chaos. Do you try to convince us of your innocence? Do you claim you can justify your actions?

There was once a time when the light of the sun shone brightly upon the prophets, and their words, sweet as honey, were shared with all people. Their wisdom spread like sunlight, bringing knowledge to the world.

But you, the cause of so much suffering, will bring both war and grief. You are the beginning of humanity's struggles and the reason for its suffering. Listen to this terrible prophecy, a warning not to be ignored.

One day, Persia will find peace, free from war and pain. On that day, a divine people, the blessed Hebrews, will pray to God. They will live near the holy city, building strong walls that will rise into the clouds.

The sounds of war will no longer fill their land. No enemy will cut them down, and the righteous will stand victorious over the wicked.

A great man will descend from heaven, a leader above all others. His hands once stretched out upon a sacred tree, the noblest of the Hebrews. He once commanded the sun to stop with his words, speaking with holiness and truth.

So do not fear, chosen people of God. Do not let the sword trouble your hearts. You are his beloved nation, his treasured light, a beautiful and noble branch of faith.

Judea, blessed and full of music, no unholy feet will trample your land again. No more will lawless invaders celebrate on your streets. Instead, your children will honor you with devotion, singing songs of praise in holy tongues.

They will bring offerings and prayers, pleasing to God. Those who endure hardship for righteousness will be rewarded.

The wicked, who spoke against heaven with their evil words, will be silenced. They will hide away, waiting for the world to be transformed.

Flames will rain down from the sky, and people will no longer harvest crops. The land will remain unplanted and untouched until humanity finally recognizes the Lord of all things, the eternal God. They will no longer worship false idols, nor honor the creatures and symbols that Egypt once taught them to revere.

The land of the righteous will be blessed. Sweet water will flow from the rocks, and streams of milk and honey will provide for the faithful. Those who trust in the one true God, the Father of all, will be rewarded for their devotion.

But why has wisdom given me this vision?

Asia, I weep for you and for the lands of the Ionians, Carians, and the gold-rich Lydians.

Sardis, your fate is sealed. Trallis, a city once loved, will fall. Laodicea, a place of beauty, will be shattered by earthquakes, reduced to dust. Darkness will spread across Asia.

The great temple of Artemis in Ephesus will be swallowed by the earth as earthquakes tear through the land. Storms will bring ruin to the sea, sinking ships and leaving Ephesus in mourning. The city will cry out in grief, searching for its lost temple, but it will be gone forever.

Then, the mighty God above will send thunderbolts down upon the wicked. Summer will replace winter in an instant, and disaster will strike. The great Thunderer will wipe out the wicked with fire, lightning, and storms. Their bodies will cover the earth, more numerous than the grains of sand on the shore.

Smyrna will mourn as it approaches the gates of Ephesus, only to meet a worse fate.

Foolish Cyme, ruined by the hands of lawless men, will fall silent forever. She will not even have a voice to cry out. She will remain lifeless, lost beneath the waters of the Cymæan streams.

The people of Cyme will suffer, forced to face the consequences of their actions. They will mourn their city, now reduced to ashes, while Lesbos sinks into the depths of the sea.

Corcyra, a city once full of joy, will be silenced forever. Hierapolis, rich and powerful, will finally receive what it desired—sorrow and endless tears. Tripolis, resting along the waters of the Mæander River, will be swallowed by the waves as God's wrath consumes it in the night.

Miletus, your time will come. A great thunderbolt will strike, bringing destruction from above. Your downfall will come because you misused the wisdom of the god you once followed.

Father of all, look kindly upon the land of Judah, a land full of fruit and prosperity. Let your people witness your justice.

For you, O God, chose this land first, giving it as a gift to humanity, entrusting its people with your divine purpose.

I long to witness the downfall of the Thracians and the destruction of the great wall between the seas, brought low like a river flowing for the fish.

Hellespont, disaster awaits you. One day, a ruler from Assyria will place a yoke across your waters. A great battle will come upon Thrace, stripping it of its strength.

A king from Egypt will take control of Macedonia. But then,

invaders from distant lands will rise against the great warriors. The Lydians, Galatians, Pamphylians, and Pisidians will bring destruction, fully armed for battle.

Italy, your time is near. You will be left in ruins, abandoned and unwept, even as your fertile lands remain untouched. A deadly plague will wipe out your people.

And then, high above in the vast heavens, the voice of God will roar like thunder, shaking the world.

The sun's flames will no longer burn, and the bright light of the moon will disappear when God takes control. Darkness will cover the earth, and people will be blinded by fear. Wild beasts and suffering will spread everywhere. This time of sorrow will last long enough for all to understand that God alone rules over everything.

On that day, God will not have mercy on those who worship false gods. People who sacrifice sheep, lambs, goats, and golden-horned bulls to lifeless idols and statues will be judged. Instead of following false beliefs, they should seek wisdom and righteousness. If they fail to love and respect the eternal God, he may destroy all the wicked and shameless people.

At the turning of the moon's cycle, a great war will spread across the world. It will be fought with deception and trickery. From the edges of the earth, a man who killed his own mother will rise to power. He will take control over all lands and rule with unmatched intelligence. He will claim what was once taken from him and bring destruction upon many. He will kill tyrants and burn everything in his path like no one before him. He will even bring back those who were afraid so they can witness his actions.

From the West, war will come, and blood will flow down hills like rushing rivers. In Macedonia, great battles will rage, and a strong force from the West will arrive. But the ruler there will meet his downfall.

Winter winds will blow as war returns to the land, filling the plains with destruction once again. Fire will rain down from the sky along with blood, water, lightning, and thick darkness. A terrible mist of war and death will cover everything, wiping out kings and powerful leaders. When this great battle finally ends, no one will fight with swords, iron, or weapons ever again. These things will no longer be allowed.

Those who survive and learn from past wickedness will finally live in peace, filled with joy.

Murderers of their own families, stop your arrogance and evil ways. In the past, you committed horrible acts—forcing young boys into terrible situations, treating young girls like slaves, and harming the innocent. In your land, even mothers lay with their own children, and daughters were forced to marry their fathers. Kings defiled themselves with wicked acts, and men engaged in unnatural behavior with animals.

You, city of sin and disgrace, will be silenced forever. The time of your celebrations will end. Virgin maidens will no longer tend the sacred fire, and your beloved temple will be reduced to ruins. I have seen with my own eyes the second great house of worship set on fire and destroyed by wicked hands. It was a house that once flourished, a sacred place built by the faithful, believed to be indestructible. But it was cast down.

No one can honor God from the grave. The wise do not worship gold, nor are they deceived by riches. Instead, they honor the one true God with pure offerings and sacrifices. But now, a wicked ruler has risen, leading a great army of powerful men. He destroyed the holy temple and left it in ruins. When he stepped onto sacred land, he defiled it. No one has ever done such a thing before.

Then, from the heavens, a great ruler will descend, blessed by God, holding a scepter in his hand. He will bring justice and return stolen riches to the good and faithful. He will destroy many cities with fire, punishing those who committed evil.

He will rebuild the city that God loves, making it shine brighter than the stars, the sun, and the moon. He will establish order and construct a holy house, pure and magnificent. A mighty tower will be built, stretching up to the clouds, visible to all people.

All those who are righteous and faithful will finally see the glory of the eternal God—a sight they have long waited for. The rising sun will shine upon this new age.

When the final days arrive, people will no longer live in fear. There will be no more betrayals, no forbidden love, no murders, and no chaos—only fairness and justice in all things. It will be the last era of the faithful, when God, the great ruler, completes His plans and establishes a glorious temple.

Babylon, once the greatest kingdom, famous for its golden throne and wealth, will fall. No longer will it stand tall by the Euphrates River. Earthquakes and destruction will bring it to ruins, and the Parthians will cause great suffering. The Chaldeans, known for their strange language, will no longer rule over the Persians and Medes. Babylon, once proud and powerful, will be judged by those it once oppressed. The very people it ruled will now bring hardship upon it.

In the end, the sea will dry up, and ships will no longer sail to Italy. Asia will be covered in water, Crete will become a flat plain, and Cyprus will face terrible suffering. The people of Paphos will cry over their great loss, and even Salamis, a once-mighty city, will be left in misery. The land will turn to barren sand along the shores, and swarms of locusts will destroy what remains of Cyprus.

When people see the fate of Tyre, they will weep. Phoenicia, your destruction is near. You will crumble into ruins so completely that even the Sirens—those who lure sailors with their songs—will mourn for you.

Five generations after Egypt's downfall, terrible events will unfold. Shameless kings will unite, and the Pamphylians will spread into Egypt, Macedonia, Asia, and Libya. A devastating war will follow, spreading madness across the world. The king of Rome and the rulers of the West will eventually put an end to the bloodshed.

A brutal winter will come, bringing heavy snow and freezing rivers and lakes. A barbaric army will invade Asia, crushing the fierce warriors of Thrace.

In their desperation, people will turn against each other, eating their own family members to survive. Wild animals will invade homes, stealing food from tables. Both beasts and birds will feast on human flesh. The sea will be filled with bodies, its waters turning red with blood. The foolish will suffer, and the earth will grow weak.

A terrible loss will come, leaving so few people that their numbers will be easy to count. They will cry out in sorrow as the sun sets, never to rise again. It will sink beneath the ocean, hiding from the wickedness it has witnessed.

A moonless night will cover the sky, and thick mist will spread across the world once more. But then, a new light from God will shine, guiding those who remained faithful and praised Him.

Isis, once worshipped as a great goddess, will be forgotten. You will be left to wander the waters of the Nile like a lost soul, and no one will remember your name.

Sarapis, once honored with temples of shining stone, will also fall into ruin. Egypt will be left in despair, and those who once followed these false gods will disappear.

Those who mourn for you will cry bitterly, but those who carry wisdom in their hearts and praise God will recognize that you were nothing.

One day, a priest dressed in linen will stand up and say, "Let us build a true and beautiful temple for God. Let us turn away from the old laws of our ancestors, for they did not realize they were worshipping gods made of stone and clay. Let us change our ways and offer praise to the one true God, the everlasting Father, the ruler of all, the giver of life."

Then, in Egypt, a great and pure temple will be built, and the people created by God will bring their offerings there. In return, God will grant them eternal life.

But when the Ethiopians turn away from the sinful Triballians and begin to settle in Egypt, they will bring corruption. In time, they will destroy the mighty temple of Egypt, fulfilling the final prophecy.

God will send his wrath upon the earth, wiping out all the wicked and foolish. No one will be spared because they did not follow what God had given them.

I saw a warning in the sky: the Sun burned fiercely among the stars, and the Moon flashed with an angry light. The stars seemed to struggle against each other as fire battled against the Sun.

Lucifer stood upon the back of Leo, ready to fight. The Moon changed shape, and Capricorn struck Taurus in the neck. Taurus blocked Capricorn from bringing back daylight. Orion broke free from his chains, and Virgo switched places with Aries, taking the fortune meant for Gemini.

The Pleiades stopped shining, and Draco abandoned its usual path.

Pisces sank into Leo's belt, and Cancer fled in fear of Orion. Scorpio moved backward into Leo, and Sirius slipped away from the Sun's light.

The great Aquarius blazed with power, while Uranus shook in fury, sending the fighting stars crashing to the earth. When they struck the ocean, flames rose, setting the entire world on fire.

The sky was left empty, with no stars remaining.

Book 6.

I speak from my heart about the great Son of the Immortal, the one praised in songs. His Father gave him a throne to rule over before he was even born. Then, in human form, he was raised up and baptized in the rushing waters of the Jordan River. As he came out of the water, escaping the fire, he was the first to see God's gentle Spirit descending like a white dove with outstretched wings.

A pure flower will bloom, and springs will overflow with water. He will guide people to the right path, showing them the way to heaven and teaching them with wisdom. He will come to bring judgment and try to convince a stubborn people, showing them that he comes from a heavenly Father.

He will walk on water, heal the sick, and raise the dead. He will remove suffering, and from a small amount of food, he will feed many.

When a child is born from the house of David, he will hold power over the entire world—earth, heaven, and sea. He will appear on earth like the first two humans, formed from each other's ribs. This will happen when the world rejoices at the birth of a child.

But for you, land of Sodom, great suffering awaits. You turned against your own God and refused to recognize Him. You crowned Him with thorns, mocking Him, and gave Him bitter gall to drink.

Because of this, great troubles will fall upon you.

Oh, blessed wood, the cross on which God was stretched—this earth will not hold you forever. You will rise again, looking toward the house of heaven, when God opens His fiery eyes and reveals His power.

Book 7.

Rhodes, you are unlucky. I grieve for you before any other, because even though you are great, you will be the first to fall. Your people will be lost, but some of your land's riches will remain.

Delos, you will drift on the sea, unstable and uncertain. Cyprus, a mighty wave will one day rise from your shining waters and sweep you away. Sicily, the fire burning beneath you will rise and consume your land.

The people will ignore the warnings sent by God.

Noah alone will survive when disaster strikes. The earth will float, mountains will drift, and even the sky will seem to shift. Everything will be covered in water, and all life will be wiped out. The winds will stop, and a new age will begin.

Phrygia, you will be the first to burn when the waters recede. You will be the first to turn away from God, choosing to follow false gods instead. But your devotion to them will only bring your own destruction.

The people of Ethiopia will suffer greatly. They will be struck down by swords, crying out in pain as they fall to the ground.

Egypt, you who thrive on the riches of the Nile, will turn against yourself. Internal conflict will tear your nation apart. In the chaos, the people will reject Apis, realizing he is not truly a god.

Laodicea, you will never see God, though you act as if you are bold and strong. A great wave from the Lycus River will crash down upon you, bringing ruin.

The mighty God will be born, performing many wonders. He will set an axle in the sky, a terrifying sign for all to see, measuring time with a pillar of fire. The burning drops will fall and destroy those who have committed great evil.

One day, there will be one ruler over all, and people will finally turn to God. But their suffering will not end completely. Everything will come to pass through the house of David, for God Himself has given power into his hands.

Under his command, messengers will rest at his feet. Some will start fires, others will call forth rivers, while some will save entire cities, and others will command the winds.

A heavy burden will weigh upon many, bringing sorrow into their hearts and changing people from within.

When a new branch grows from its roots, creation will once again flourish, providing food for all. The world will be full, but the rulers of that time will be warlike Persians, and their actions will bring terror.

Mothers will take their own sons as husbands, and sons will bring ruin upon their mothers. Daughters will lie with their fathers, breaking the laws of nature.

But then, Rome's warriors will strike with their spears, and blood will flood the land. The leader of Italy will be forced to flee, but his army will leave behind a golden lance, a symbol of their rule, carried by the strongest fighters.

When the ill-fated city of Ilium is finally destroyed, it will not be a place of weddings but of graves. Brides will weep in sorrow, for they did not know God, but instead celebrated with loud music, beating drums and clashing cymbals.

Colophon, seek wisdom from the oracles, for a great fire looms over you.

Thessaly, your land will vanish, and even your ashes will be lost. You will be torn away from the mainland, drifting like wreckage. War will leave you broken, washed away by rushing rivers and swords.

Corinth, your fate is grim. The god of war will surround you, and your people will destroy each other.

Tyre, you will be left abandoned and alone. Once strong, you will be brought to ruin, like a widow grieving the loss of her people.

Cœle-Syria, last stronghold of the Phoenicians, the sea of Berytus will crash upon you. You are doomed because you did not recognize your God—the one who was baptized in the Jordan River while the Spirit descended like a dove upon him. He existed before the earth and the stars, born from the Father, and took on human flesh through the Holy Spirit. He returned quickly to his Father's house in heaven.

Three great towers were built in heaven, where God's noble guides—Hope, Faith, and Reverence—dwell. They do not find joy in gold or silver but in the righteous acts of people, in sacrifices and pure thoughts.

You will worship the eternal and mighty God, not by burning incense or sacrificing lambs, but by offering prayers with your people. You will release birds into the sky as a sign, sprinkling pure water on the fire, saying:

"As the Father created you, the Word, I send forth this bird as a messenger of my prayers, just as you revealed yourself through fire and water."

You must never turn away a stranger in need. When a hungry traveler arrives at your door, welcome him, sprinkle him with water, and pray three times. Say to God:

"I do not seek wealth. I once received a stranger as a guest, just as I now stand before you, my provider, asking for your mercy."

After praying, give to the traveler, and let him go in peace.

Do not cause suffering, and remain pure in heart and faith. Let the fear of God guide you.

Sardinia, once strong, will turn to ashes. It will no longer be an island when the tenth age comes. Sailors will search for it, but it will be gone, and seabirds will cry over its disappearance.

Mygdonia, trapped by the sea, you will exist for many ages, but in the end, a scorching wind will destroy you, bringing countless sorrows.

Celtic lands, high in the mountains beyond the Alps, deep sand will bury you completely. You will no longer provide grain or livestock, and ice will cover your land, punishing you for the wrongs you failed to recognize.

Mighty Rome, you will send out lightning-like power after the Macedonian spears, but God will make you disappear when you believe yourself to be strongest. You will suffer and cry out in agony.

Rome, I warn you once more—your downfall is certain, and you will not stand forever.

Syria, I grieve for you. Your future is filled with suffering, and I mourn what is to come.

O people of Thebes, you do not see the danger ahead. A terrible sound is coming, while flutes play their tunes.

A trumpet will blast a warning, and you will witness your land being destroyed.

Woe to you, suffering city! Woe to the raging sea! Fire will consume you completely, and the saltwater will bring destruction to your people.

A great fire will spread across the earth like a flood, burning everything in its path. The mountains will be set ablaze, rivers will dry up, and springs will vanish.

The world will fall into chaos as people perish. Those who are burned will look up, but instead of stars, they will see only fire in the sky.

Their suffering will not end quickly. Their bodies will waste away, and their spirits will burn for many years. Then, they will understand that God's law is not to be tested or ignored.

The earth will be filled with suffering because people worshipped false gods and filled their altars with lies.

Those who tell false prophecies for money will face great pain. The Hebrews, dressed in rough sheep's wool, will also prove false. They will not receive what they expected, but instead, they will change their ways and no longer mislead the righteous—those who truly worship God with their hearts.

After many years, in a new era, the world will change.

Darkness will cover everything, and the night will be long and without light. A horrible stench of burning sulfur will fill the air, signaling the deaths of many, who will perish by violence and starvation.

Then, God will create a pure mind in people and restore the world to how it was meant to be.

No one will need to plow fields, and no oxen will pull the plow. There will be no need for crops or vineyards, because all people will eat together from the food God provides, like sweet manna from heaven.

And God will live among them, teaching them, just as he has taught me.

I have done many terrible things, some knowingly and some in ignorance.

I lived a life of selfishness, ignoring the laws of marriage and breaking sacred oaths.

I turned away those in need and followed my own desires, ignoring God's words.

Because of this, fire has consumed me, and I will suffer.

I will not live forever, but in time, my punishment will come. By the sea, people will build a tomb for me, and I will be stoned to death.

For I have committed a terrible sin—bringing forth a son by my own father.

Strike me down! End my life! Only then will I be able to lift my eyes toward heaven.

Book 8.

God's warnings of great anger and destruction in the final days will come upon an unfaithful world. I reveal these things to all people, speaking to every city.

From the time when the great tower fell and human speech was divided into many languages, different kingdoms rose to power. First was Egypt, then Persia, Media, Ethiopia, Assyria, and Babylon. After them came the proud rule of Macedonia. Finally, the fifth and last kingdom, that of the Italians, will bring great suffering upon the earth.

It will force people from all nations into its control, create laws for many, and claim power over all things.

But even the strongest rule will not last forever. God's justice may take time, but in the end, everything will be reduced to dust. Fire will destroy all things, burning even the highest mountains and consuming every living being.

The root of all evil is greed and foolishness. People will love gold and silver more than anything else. They will treasure wealth above the light of the sun, the sky, the sea, or the land that provides them with food. They will forget God, the true giver of all things, the Father of all. Faith and kindness will be ignored.

Greed will bring chaos, turning families against each other. With money as their guide, people will no longer honor marriage. Lands and seas will be divided, guarded by those who serve the wealthy. The powerful will take from the hardworking, pretending it is fair, while expanding their own wealth.

If the earth were not placed far from the heavens, even the light would be bought and sold. The rich would claim the sun itself, and God would have to create another world for the poor.

But Rome, your time will come. A punishment from above will strike you. You will be the first to fall, brought low and turned to ruins. Fire will consume you, reducing your streets to ashes. Your treasures will be lost, and wild animals will take over your empty foundations. You will be completely abandoned, as if you had never existed.

Where will your sacred statues be then? What god will save you— gold, stone, or bronze idols? Where will your rulers and laws go? Where will the proud bloodline of your gods—Rhea, Cronus, and Zeus—be? You worshipped lifeless images of the dead, giving honor to forgotten graves, while Crete foolishly took pride in these empty tombs.

Rome will have fifteen rulers who spread their power from the east to the west, enslaving nations. Then, an old man, whose name is tied to the sea, will rise. He will travel the world, gathering wealth, stealing gold and silver wherever he can.

He will take part in false religious rituals, declare his child to be a god, and erase all sacred things. He will expose old lies for what they are. But his own time will come, and his death will bring sorrow to the land.

People will see that destruction is near. They will realize that Rome's strength is crumbling. Parents and children will cry out together, mourning along the banks of the Tiber River, knowing the end is near.

After him, in the final days, three rulers will rise. Their names will reflect the power of God, who rules now and forever. One of them, an old man, will hold the throne for a long time. He will store up the world's wealth, preparing for the return of a fugitive who once killed his own mother. When that man comes back from the farthest parts of the earth, the old ruler will distribute his riches and make Asia prosperous.

Then, Rome, you will mourn. You will take off your royal robes and wear clothes of sorrow. Your pride will be gone, and you will never rise again. The mighty legions that once carried the eagle into battle will fall.

Where will your power be then? What lands will still follow your reckless rule? The whole world will be in chaos when the Almighty comes to judge the living and the dead.

Families will turn against each other. Parents and children will no longer love one another because of their faithlessness and suffering. You will face grinding despair, your cities will fall, and the earth will shake and split open.

A fiery dragon with glowing eyes and a full belly will rise from the sea, bringing destruction. Your people will suffer famine and civil war. When that happens, the end of the world will be near. The final day of judgment will come, and God will choose those who are worthy.

The wrath of God will strike Rome first. There will be endless bloodshed, and life will become unbearable.

Oh, foolish and reckless nation, you never understood where you came from or where you are going. You entered this world naked and unworthy, and you will return to nothingness before facing judgment for your unjust rule.

A mighty force will come down from the heavens, and you will be cast deep into the earth. Flames, burning oil, and sulfur will consume you. You will vanish into fire and become dust for eternity. Those who see it will hear the cries of suffering rising from the depths of the underworld—shouts of grief and teeth grinding in pain.

In death, there is no difference between rich and poor. Everyone leaves the earth as empty-handed as they arrived. There will be no kings, rulers, or tyrants. No judges will take bribes. No blood will be poured on altars. There will be no drums, no flutes, no wild dancing, no music of harps or trumpets calling to war. The dead do not fight or argue. They do not carry swords.

The afterlife is a prison, locked for eternity, waiting for God's final judgment.

Rome, your golden idols will not save you. You will face your first punishment, and your people will weep and grind their teeth in agony. No longer will Greeks, Syrians, or any foreign nation bow to your rule. Instead, you will be plundered and forced to suffer the same oppression you once inflicted on others. You will be left in ruins, a shameful reminder to the world.

Then, the sixth generation of Latin rulers will come to an end, and their line will disappear. A new king from the same land will rise, ruling over every nation. He will have full power, and his descendants will continue to rule, as destined by God.

Time will continue moving forward, and when Egypt has been ruled by fifteen kings, a great event will take place.

The era of the Phoenix will come to an end, and a fierce, chaotic army will rise against the Hebrews. War will rage, and Rome's pride will finally be shattered.

Rome's power will fall even while it still seems strong. Once a mighty queen among cities, it will no longer thrive when a ruler from Asia arrives, bringing war. After he has completed his conquests, he will come to the city.

When Rome has ruled for 348 years, disaster will strike. The city will be taken by force, and its name will be erased. I, so full of sorrow, wonder if I will live to see the day of Rome's destruction—a day that will bring the greatest suffering to the Latin people.

A leader with a fiery spirit will come from Asia, riding in a Trojan chariot and hiding his children. When he cuts through the land and crosses the sea, destruction will follow. Blood will spill as the mighty empire falls. A dog will chase a lion, and the shepherds will be destroyed. His power will be taken from him, and he will descend into the underworld.

Rhodes will suffer its worst disaster. Thebes will fall under cruel rule. Egypt will collapse under corrupt leaders.

A man who somehow escapes this destruction will be truly blessed. Rome will be reduced to ruins. Delos will lose its beauty, and Samos will turn to sand.

Pride will bring disaster upon the Persians, and their arrogance will be crushed.

Then, the holy ruler of the world will raise the dead and take control forever. Rome will face three terrible punishments from God. People will be destroyed by their own actions because they refused to listen and change their ways.

When famine, plague, and violent war increase, the former ruler will call the senate and plan even greater destruction.

The earth will bloom again, and rainstorms, fire, and strong winds will sweep over the land. But people will continue in their shameless ways, ignoring the warnings of both God and men. They will follow greedy and corrupt rulers, seeking wealth without end. They will lie, betray, and destroy faith, showing no sense of right or wrong.

In time, the stars will fall into the sea, one by one. A brilliant comet will appear in the sky, a warning of the war and suffering to come.

I do not want to live when a wicked woman rules. But the day will come when divine grace reigns, and a holy child will defeat the great destroyer of mankind. The depths of the earth will be opened, and suddenly, the world will be covered.

When the tenth generation has passed into the underworld, a woman will rise to power. Her rule will bring hardship, and God will allow even greater suffering.

The sun will grow dim, shining weakly even at night. The stars will disappear, and great storms will shake the earth.

Then, the dead will rise. The lame will run, the deaf will hear, the blind will see, and the mute will speak. Life and wealth will be shared among all people.

The land will not be divided by walls or fences, and it will produce more than ever before. Streams of sweet wine, milk, and honey will flow freely.

Then, the judgment of God will come.

Seasons will change—the winter will bring summer. When God decides, all prophecies will be fulfilled, and the world will come to an end.

When the time of judgment comes, the earth will tremble and sweat. From heaven, the eternal King will appear to judge all people and the entire world.

Both the faithful and the unfaithful will see God standing with the saints at the end of time. He will judge every soul, and the world will become empty and covered in thorns. People will throw away their idols and wealth, realizing they are worthless.

A great fire will consume the earth, the sky, and the sea, even breaking open the gates of the underworld. The dead will rise and stand in the light alongside the saints, but the wicked will be trapped in the fire, suffering for eternity.

Every secret will be revealed, as God will expose the hidden thoughts of all people. Many will cry out in sorrow, grinding their teeth in regret. The sun will darken, the stars will stop shining, and the sky will be rolled up like a scroll. The moon's light will fade, mountains will be flattened, and hills will disappear. The earth will become level, and the seas will vanish. Rivers and springs will dry up as the world is scorched by intense heat.

A trumpet will sound from heaven, filling the world with a terrifying noise, warning of the suffering to come. The ground will split open, revealing the depths of the underworld, and all kings will stand before God's judgment seat. Fire and burning sulfur will pour down from the heavens.

A great sign will appear—a holy symbol recognized by believers, but rejected by the world. It will bring light to those who follow the truth and mark the faithful with its power. Twelve springs of water will flow, and a strong shepherd will guide the people with an iron staff.

The hidden message written in acrostics reveals the name of the Saviour, the immortal King who suffered for the sake of the world.

Moses foreshadowed him when he lifted his hands in faith, helping his people win the battle against Amalek. This showed that he was chosen and honored by his Father, God.

He is the rod of David, the promised foundation. Those who believe in him will have eternal life.

He will not come in glory but as a humble man, without honor or beauty, to bring hope to those who suffer. He will restore the beauty of human life and bring faith to those who have none. He will give new life to the first man, who was created by God's hands but was led astray by the serpent's deception, bringing death and the knowledge of good and evil. Turning away from God, humanity followed its own ways instead.

From the beginning, the Almighty spoke to his Son, saying, "Let us create mankind in our image." God shaped them with his hands, and in time, the Son would bring them back to their true form. Keeping this promise, he will enter the world, born of a holy virgin, and he will be baptized with water by the hands of elders. Through his words, he will perform miracles and heal every sickness.

With just his voice, he will calm the wind, and with his footsteps, he will bring peace to the raging sea. From five loaves and a fish, he will feed five thousand people in the desert, gathering twelve baskets of leftovers as a sign of hope for all nations.

He will call upon the souls of the faithful and show love to those who suffer. Though he will be mocked, beaten, and rejected, he will repay evil with kindness, embracing a life of humility. He sees and hears all, searching the hearts of people and revealing the truth. He is the Word that created all things, and through him, even the dead will rise, and every sickness will be healed.

But in the end, he will be handed over to cruel and faithless men. They will strike him with their hands and spit on him with mouths filled with hatred. He will be whipped and remain silent, revealing nothing about himself, even as they mock him.

They will place a crown of thorns upon his head, for the thorns are a symbol of his eternal kingship. They will pierce his side with a reed, fulfilling the law, though their hearts are ruled by anger and revenge.

When all these things happen, every law written by men will be fulfilled. He will stretch out his hands, embracing the whole world. But instead of kindness, they will give him gall for food and vinegar to drink. The curtain in the temple will tear in two, and in the middle of the day, darkness will cover the earth for three hours.

The old way of worship, hidden behind rituals and traditions, will no longer be needed when the Eternal One walks among people. He will enter the depths of the underworld, bringing hope to the faithful and announcing the end of time. He will fall asleep in death, but on the third day, he will rise again, breaking the power of death.

Emerging from the grave, he will be the first to show the way to resurrection. He will cleanse people's sins with the waters of life, so they may be reborn and no longer enslaved to the ways of the world.

First, he will appear to his followers in the flesh, just as before. The marks of his suffering will remain on his hands and feet, representing the four corners of the world. The leaders of the earth will have carried out a terrible and unjust act against him.

Rejoice, daughter of Zion, for though you have suffered, your King is coming! He will arrive humbly, riding on a young donkey. He will break the heavy chains of oppression and set people free from unjust laws and burdens.

Know your God, the Son of God. Honor him, keep him in your heart, and love him with all your soul. Praise his name and turn away from your old ways. Wash yourself clean of the sins of the past. He is not pleased by songs or prayers alone, nor does he care for sacrifices of things that perish. Instead, offer him a sincere heart and true understanding. When you do, you will see the Father.

Then, the world will be left in silence. The air, the land, the sea, and the light of the sky will stand still. Day and night will blend together into emptiness. The stars will fall from the sky. Birds will no longer fly, and animals will disappear. No voices of people, birds, or creatures will be heard. The world will be without sound, except for the deep sea roaring in anger. The creatures of the ocean will die, and no ships will sail the waves.

The earth will be soaked in blood from endless wars. People will cry out in pain, grinding their teeth in fear and suffering. Hunger, thirst, disease, and violence will consume them. They will wish for death, but it will not come. There will be no rest, no night to bring relief. They will cry out to God for help, but he will turn away, for he gave them many chances to repent.

God has shown me all of this, and everything I have spoken will come to pass. I know the number of grains of sand, the depths of the sea, the hidden places of the earth, and the darkness of the underworld. I know the stars, the trees, every living creature, and every person— those who have lived, those who live now, and those yet to be born. I gave people the ability to think, see, and hear. I understand even the silent thoughts of the heart.

I know everything, from the beginning to the end. I alone am God, and there is no other. But people carve statues from wood and call them gods. They shape them with their hands and bow before them, singing praises to lifeless idols and performing meaningless rituals.

People turned away from their Creator and became slaves to sin. Even though they had everything they needed, they wasted their gifts on things that could not help them. They offered sacrifices to lifeless idols, burning flesh and bones as if it were for their own dead. They poured out blood on altars for demons and lit fires in my name, thinking I needed light. They foolishly believed I was thirsty, offering wine to statues that could not drink or save them.

I do not need your burnt offerings, your incense, or your sacrifices of blood. These rituals were created in honor of kings and tyrants, not for me. They worship false gods, calling lifeless statues divine while forgetting the Creator who gave them life. They put their trust in things that cannot see or hear, completely blind to what is truly good.

I gave people two paths—one leading to life and the other to death—and I warned them to choose the path of goodness. But they ran toward destruction, bringing eternal fire upon themselves.

People were made in my image, with reason and wisdom. Instead of offering bloody sacrifices, prepare a pure table. Feed the hungry, give water to the thirsty, clothe those in need, and help those who suffer. Support the weak and provide kindness, for that is the true sacrifice I desire. If you do this, I will reward you with eternal light and a life that never fades when I cleanse the world with fire.

I will test everything, separating what is pure from what is corrupt. I will roll up the heavens, open the depths of the earth, and raise the dead. I will end fate and destroy the power of death. Then I will bring judgment, testing both the righteous and the wicked. I will separate the faithful from the unfaithful, just as a shepherd separates sheep from goats. Those who sought power and silenced the righteous will be cast out.

No longer will anyone worry about tomorrow or dwell on the past. Time will not be measured by days, seasons, or sunsets. Instead, I will create a never-ending day filled with the light that my people have longed for.

You, the eternal and pure one, measure the power of storms and command the lightning. You calm the roar of thunder and control the raging winds. You hold back the fire of destruction and soften the blows of harsh weather. You know everything that will happen and decide what is good.

Your Son, who has always been with you, agrees with your will. Together, you created life and gave humans breath. You said, "Let us make man in our image and give him dominion over the world." And so, by your word, everything was made—the heavens, the air, the fire, the earth, the sea, the sun, the moon, and the stars.

Both day and night, in sleep and while awake, in spirit and thought, in strength and wisdom, all living creatures—those that swim, fly, walk, or crawl—were created by his will, following your guidance.

In the last days, he passed through the earth, coming from the womb of the virgin Mary. A new light appeared, and from heaven, he took on human form. First, the angel Gabriel came in his shining presence and spoke to the young woman, saying,

"O pure virgin, receive God into your heart."

As he spoke, he brought God's grace upon her. She was filled with fear and amazement at his words, trembling with surprise. Her heart raced, and she was overwhelmed. But soon, she felt comforted, her heart was lifted, and she smiled with joy. A soft blush appeared on her face, and she felt a sense of wonder and humility.

Then, the Word entered her womb, and in time, he took on flesh and life, becoming a human child through a miraculous birth. This was a great wonder for the world, but not for God the Father or God the Son.

The earth rejoiced at his birth, the heavens celebrated, and the world was filled with joy. A new star appeared in the sky as a sign, and wise men honored it. The newborn child was revealed in a humble manger to those who followed God—shepherds, goatherds, and those who cared for the flocks. Bethlehem, chosen by God, became the birthplace of the Word.

Live with humility in your heart. Reject cruelty and love your neighbor as yourself. Serve God with all your soul.

We, who come from the holy line of Christ, are called as one family, united in faith. We live in truth and righteousness. We do not enter the temples of false gods, offer sacrifices to idols, or worship lifeless images with prayers, incense, or candles. We do not bring offerings of bulls or shed the blood of animals as if such things could erase sin. We do not burn the flesh of sacrifices, sending foul smoke into the sky.

Instead, we worship with pure hearts, filled with love and kindness. With joyful songs and praise, we honor you, the eternal and true Father of all, full of wisdom and light.

Book 11.

O people of the world, scattered far and wide, living in great cities and powerful nations, spread across the east, west, north, and south, speaking many different languages and ruled by many kings—I must tell you of terrible things to come.

A long time ago, after the great flood wiped out the first people, God created a new race of humans. But they became proud and tried to build a tower so high that it would reach heaven. In his anger, God confused their languages and brought chaos upon them, causing them to fight among themselves. Since then, ten generations of people have lived on earth, spreading across different lands and forming separate nations.

First, Egypt will rise to power, ruling with justice. Wise men will govern the land, but eventually, a fierce and ruthless leader will take control. His name will be marked by the first letter of an acrostic, and he will use his sword against those who remain faithful to God.

During his rule, a great sign will appear in Egypt—one that will bring hope. Crops will grow in abundance, saving people from terrible famine. A great lawgiver, once a prisoner, will come from the east, born from the people of Assyria. His name will carry the number ten.

When Egypt is struck by ten great plagues sent from heaven, I will speak again of these things.

Memphis, a great city, will suffer destruction. The waters of the Red Sea will swallow many of its people.

Then, when the twelve tribes of Israel leave the land of Egypt as God commands, the Almighty will give them laws to guide all of humanity. A mighty king will rise to rule over them, a strong and noble leader whose name will be linked to Egypt and Thebes. Though he will pretend to be kind, he will be a dangerous ruler, watching over his people while preparing for war.

After twelve generations, lasting over seven hundred years, Persia will take control. Then, suffering will fall upon the Jewish people—a time of terrible famine and disease that they will not escape.

A Persian king will rule, and after him, his grandson will inherit the throne. But when 549 years have passed, Persia will collapse, and its people will become slaves to the Medes. They will suffer greatly in battles and be struck down by their enemies.

Disaster will come quickly to the Persians, Assyrians, Egyptians, Libyans, Ethiopians, Carians, Pamphylians, and many others.

A ruler will pass his power to his grandsons, who will take control of the entire world, stealing from many nations without mercy. The Persians will mourn by the Tigris River, and Egypt will weep as its people suffer.

Then, a wealthy man from India will bring destruction to the land of the Medes. The people of Media will pay for their past sins and will be forced to serve Ethiopian rulers for 107 years, carrying heavy burdens under their rule.

After this, an Indian king with dark skin and gray hair will take power. He will be a strong and determined leader, bringing terrible wars to the East. His rule will be harsh, and he will wipe out many people. For 30 years, he will hold his throne, and after 17 more, nations will rise against him, seeking freedom. For three years, they will fight for their independence. But he will return, forcing all the nations back under his control, making them serve him once again. Afterward, peace will spread across the world.

Then, a great Assyrian king will rise, a leader who will persuade people to follow the laws of God. The most powerful rulers will fear him and submit to his wisdom because he will rule with understanding and fairness. He will rebuild the temple of God and destroy idols, bringing people together, including the elderly and young children. His name will carry the number 200 and a sign of the 18th letter.

For 25 years, he will lead, but when his time ends, many kings will rise—one for each tribe, city, island, and land. Among them, one will be greater than the rest, ruling over the other kings and their descendants for 80 years before their time ends.

When a fierce and violent ruler appears, bringing war, destruction will return to the Persian land. The rivers will run red with blood when a stronger conqueror arrives.

Italy will bring forth a new ruler, a powerful force that will shock the world. There will be the cries of young children near a pure spring in a dark cave, born from a wild beast that feeds on sheep. As they grow, they will build a mighty city upon seven hills and lead wars, destroying many people. Their names will become a great sign for future generations.

They will construct great walls around their city and fight many wars. In Egypt, there will be rebellion and suffering, as I have warned before. A terrible disaster will strike Egyptian homes, and once again, its people will turn against each other.

I grieve for you, Phrygia. A conqueror from Greece, known for taming horses, will invade your land, bringing war and disease.

Troy, I pity you. From Sparta, a powerful and vengeful woman will come to your city, bringing ruin. She will bring endless suffering, filling your streets with pain and sorrow. When the Greeks attack, the bravest warriors will rise to battle, and among them, a strong king will fight for his brother, carrying out terrible acts.

The mighty walls of Troy will fall. After ten long years of bloody war, a clever trick will bring its downfall. A great wooden structure will be taken into the city, but the Trojans will not realize it hides Greek warriors inside. That night, disaster will strike. So many lives will be lost in a single night, and an old man will weep over the destruction. But even in ruin, Troy's name will live on in history.

A great hero, born from Zeus, will have a name beginning with the first letter of the alphabet. He will return home in triumph, only to be betrayed and killed by a deceitful woman.

Then, a new leader will rise from the bloodline of Assaracus, a strong and brave man. He will escape the fires of Troy, carrying his elderly father on his shoulders and leading his son by the hand. As he flees, he will carefully avoid the raging flames and pass through the dangers of both land and sea. His name will have three syllables, and the first letter of the alphabet will mark him as an important figure.

He will establish a city for the powerful Latin people, but in his fifteenth year, he will meet his end, drowning in the sea. Even in death, he will not be forgotten, and his descendants will go on to rule vast lands stretching to the Euphrates and Tigris rivers, across the heart of the Assyrian kingdom and the lands of the Parthians.

A wise old man, a great poet, will also arise. He will be known for his knowledge and wisdom, writing incredible stories that will shape the world. Some of his words will even come from my own verses. He will reveal my books but then hide them away, keeping them secret until the final days of life and death.

When these events unfold, the Greeks will once again fight among themselves. The Assyrians, Arabs, Medes, Persians, Sicilians, Lydians, Thracians, and Egyptians will all be drawn into war. Chaos will spread across the lands, and God will bring confusion to all nations.

A ruthless leader from Assyria, with the heart of a beast, will rise to power. Cunning and brutal, he will cross every land and sea, striking down all in his path. Greece, once strong, will suffer greatly.

For 78 years, Greece will endure war and suffering, reduced to ruins as it becomes the battlefield for many nations.

Then, a Macedonian ruler will rise, bringing even more pain to Greece. He will destroy Thrace, the islands, and the warlike Triballi. A powerful warrior, he will bear a name linked to the number 500. His rule will be short, but he will leave behind the greatest empire on earth. However, he will meet his end by a soldier's spear while believing he was safe.

His son, a strong-willed child, will take the throne. His name will start with the first letter of the alphabet, but his dynasty will not last. Though some will claim he is the son of Zeus or Ammon, he will not be seen as their true heir.

This ruler will lead many wars, seizing cities and bringing suffering to countless people. His conquests will leave a deep wound on Europe. He will devastate Babylon and every land under the sun, becoming the only man to conquer both the East and the West.

Oh, Babylon, your time of glory is over. Once called a queen, you will now serve the victories of others. War will come upon Asia, bringing great destruction. Your people will suffer, and many will be slain.

A powerful warrior, known by the number four, will rise. He will be skilled with the spear, fearsome in battle, and deadly with the bow and arrow. But soon after, famine and war will spread across Cilicia and Assyria. Kings will fight each other, consumed by endless conflict.

You must flee from your former ruler—do not stay, but do not be afraid to leave. A terrible beast, like a raging lion, will appear. He will be a brutal leader, cruel and without justice, wearing a cloak upon his shoulders. Stay away from the man who wields thunder as his weapon. All of Asia will fall under harsh rule, and the land will be soaked in blood.

A powerful leader from Pella will establish a mighty city in Egypt, named after himself. But despite his greatness, he will meet his end, betrayed by his own companions. This leader will be murdered at a feast after leaving India and returning to Babylon.

After him, other rulers will rise—cruel, selfish men who will devour their people. They will each rule over their own tribes, but none will bring peace. Then, a mighty leader will come, uniting all of Europe. However, after much bloodshed, he will surrender to fate and die.

Following him, eight rulers will come from the same family, all sharing the same name.

At this time, a queen from Egypt will rise to power. She will rule a great city, Alexandria, the pride of the Macedonian empire. It will shine brightly as the center of civilization. But Memphis will resent her rule. There will be peace in the world, and Egypt will become more fertile than ever, bringing forth abundant crops.

However, disaster will strike the Jewish people. They will face famine and an unbearable plague with no escape. But Egypt, with its rich land, will provide refuge for many wandering souls.

Egypt will have eight kings, ruling for 233 years. But their family line will not last. A woman will rise, bringing ruin to the kingdom, betraying her people. One by one, the rulers will fall—fathers killed by sons, and sons murdered before they can bear their own children. Yet, a new ruler will eventually emerge, and a new dynasty will grow.

A queen will take the throne, ruling over the Nile, which flows into the sea through seven streams. Her name will have the number twenty. She will demand great riches, gathering gold and silver. But her own people will betray her. Egypt will once again be thrown into war, filled with bloodshed and destruction.

Meanwhile, Rome will be ruled by many leaders, none of them truly great. Tyrants will take power, with thousands of rulers and countless officials controlling the laws and assemblies. The mightiest emperors, known as Caesars, will govern, but they will all meet tragic fates.

The last of these emperors will have a name marked by the number ten. He will fall to war, struck down by an enemy. The young men of Rome will carry his body and bury him with honor, offering tributes in his memory.

When 620 years have passed since Rome's founding by its legendary ruler, no longer will dictators rule for fixed terms. Instead, a single ruler will take full control, a king who will be seen as equal to the gods.

Then, Egypt, prepare for the king who will come to you. A fierce warrior with a shining helmet will arrive, bringing war.

You, once powerful, will be conquered and left defenseless. Battles will rage around your cities, bringing destruction. After suffering greatly in these wars, you will be forced to submit, unable to resist. In the end, you will join with a powerful ruler, bound together in an unwanted union.

Oh, unfortunate bride, you will surrender your kingdom to the Roman ruler. You will pay for everything you once did when you ruled with strength. Your entire land, stretching to Libya and the lands of dark-skinned people, will be given to this unstoppable leader as part of your dowry.

No longer will you stand alone, for you will be joined to a ruthless warrior—a brutal, merciless conqueror. But this will not bring you happiness. You will be forgotten, your name lost among the people. Your once-proud legacy will vanish, and a tomb will encircle you, a resting place for a ruler who has fallen.

A great crowd will mourn you, and even the mighty king will grieve your passing.

Then, Egypt, you will become a servant, forced to bear the burden of war against the Indian lands. You will be ruled harshly, and the Nile will flow with your sorrow like endless tears. Though once a land of riches, feeding great cities, you will now provide for cruel invaders, men who show no mercy.

Oh, wealthy Egypt, how many invaders will claim you as their prize? Once home to powerful rulers, you will now be a slave to foreign nations. You will suffer for what you once did to others—when you enslaved a people who worshiped God, forcing them to toil under the sun, breaking their backs for your wealth. You made them cry tears that watered your fields.

Because of this, the eternal God, who rules from heaven, will bring judgment upon you. You will pay for the wrongs you committed long ago, and only then will you understand that God's wrath has fallen upon you.

Now, I will go to Python and Panopeus, cities with great towers, where people will finally recognize that my words are true. They will no longer doubt my prophecies.

When you read these words, do not be afraid. Everything that is to come, and everything that has already happened, will be revealed. Then, no one will say that this prophecy was given by chance.

Lord, let this be the end of my song. Take away the madness that fills my voice and replace it with a song of peace.

Book 12.

Listen now to the sorrowful days that will come for the people of Latium.

First, after the kings of Egypt have fallen and been buried in the earth, and after the man from Pella, who ruled over both the East and West, has died—his body abandoned by Babylon, proving false the claims that he was the son of Zeus—there will come a ruler from the bloodline of Assaracus, a descendant of Troy. He will survive great destruction and fire.

Many rulers will follow—some great warriors, others young and inexperienced. After six hundred and twenty years of Rome's rule, the first great leader from across the western sea will take control. He will be a powerful and warlike ruler whose name begins with the first letter of the alphabet. He will conquer lands rich in food and bring devastation through war. The lands he conquers will pay for the wrongs they have done.

This great warrior will be the strongest in battle. Thrace and Sicily will submit to him, and Memphis will fall, its downfall caused by corrupt leaders and a powerful, independent woman who will die by the sword. He will establish laws for the people and bring everything under his control. His rule will be long and filled with great fame, and no king before or after him will be greater.

During his time, the world will witness signs—marvelous seasons and wonders on the earth. And when a bright star, shining like the sun, appears in the sky at midday, the hidden Word of the Most High will come down, taking human form. The power of Rome and its people will grow stronger. But in time, this mighty king will die, passing his rule to another.

The next ruler will be a strong warrior, wearing a purple cloak. His name will carry the number three hundred, and he will lead great battles. He will defeat the Medes and the Parthians, who fight with arrows. He will bring destruction to the great city, and Egypt, Assyria, and distant lands near the Rhine will suffer under his rule. He will also attack a city near the river Eridanus, known for its evil schemes. But in the end, he will be struck down by a shining blade.

After him will come a cunning ruler, whose name carries the number three. He will amass great wealth, but his greed will have no limits. He will continue taking more and more from the earth, never satisfied. However, there will be a time of peace, and wars will cease. He will seek wisdom through divination, hoping to secure his rule. But a great sign will appear—while he is dying, small drops of blood will fall from the sky.

He will bring great suffering to the people of Rome, committing terrible crimes. He will kill the leaders of the assembly and cause a severe shortage of food. The people of Cappadocia, Thrace, Macedonia, and Italy will struggle through a devastating famine.

Egypt will be the only land able to feed many people. Meanwhile, a deceitful king will secretly harm an innocent young woman. The people, filled with sorrow, will give her a proper burial and turn against the king, plotting against him in anger. While Rome is still strong, this ruler will fall.

A new leader will take power, marked by the number twenty. He will bring war and suffering to the Sauromatians, Thracians, and the Triballi, fierce warriors known for their skill with spears. Rome will spread destruction, and a terrifying sign will appear when this ruler governs Italy and Pannonia. At midday, darkness will cover the sky, and stones will fall from heaven. Soon after, the ruler of Italy will meet his fate and die.

Then, a new leader, known by the number fifty, will rise. He will bring destruction to the wealthy and powerful, acting like a venomous serpent spreading war. He will even bring harm to his own family and cause chaos everywhere. As a chariot racer, he will take part in deadly contests, spilling blood and leaving destruction behind. He will cut through the land between two seas, staining it with blood. But in the end, he will disappear, only to return, claiming to be a god. However, the true God will prove him powerless.

During his reign, peace will come for a time, and people will live without fear. Water will flow through the land, creating new paths. The ruler will organize grand games and contests, even competing himself, singing and playing music. Eventually, he will abandon his throne and die far from home, facing the consequences of his actions.

After him, three rulers will rise. Two of them will have names linked to the number seventy, and another will be connected to the third letter of the alphabet. They will meet violent ends in different places, falling in battle. Then, a mighty warrior, known by the number seventy, will take power. He will bring suffering to the faithful, leading brutal campaigns against Phoenicia and Assyria. His armies will bring war to the sacred land of Solyma and reach the shores of the Tiber.

Phoenicia will suffer greatly, bound by its own victories, and other nations will trample over it. Assyria will fall, and its people, including children and wives, will be taken as captives by foreign rulers. Their wealth and way of life will be destroyed. God's wrath will come upon them for abandoning His laws and worshipping false gods. Wars, famine, and disease will spread across the land.

Eventually, this merciless king will face his fate. After him, two rulers will take power, honoring their great father. They will become warriors, leading armies and continuing the fight. One of them will be a noble leader, whose name equals three hundred, but he will be betrayed and killed—not in battle, but by treachery in Rome.

Then, a ruler marked by the number four will take control. He will be beloved across the world, bringing peace. Nations from the west to the east will willingly follow him, and cities will submit to his rule without force. The world will rest from war, and he will be blessed by the Almighty God.

However, famine will strike Pannonia and the lands of the Celts, taking many lives. In Assyria, where the Orontes River flows, great buildings will rise, admired by the powerful ruler. But his trust in others will lead to his downfall—he will be wounded in his own palace, betrayed by a friend, and die unexpectedly.

After him, another ruler will rise, linked to the number fifty. He will bring destruction to Rome, taking the lives of many citizens, though his reign will be short. His fate will be sealed because of a past ruler's actions.

Then, a new leader, known by the number three hundred, will take the throne. He will launch fierce attacks on Thrace, Germany, and Iberia, spreading destruction. The Jews will suffer another great tragedy, and Phoenicia will be soaked in blood. The walls of Assyria will crumble as invaders tear through the land, leaving behind ruin and death. Finally, another ruthless ruler will rise, bringing even more devastation.

Then, disasters from the mighty God will come—earthquakes, plagues, unexpected snowstorms, and powerful lightning strikes will affect every land.

A great Celtic king, who roams the mountains, will meet an unfortunate end as he eagerly rushes into battle. Worn out from war, he will fall, and foreign soil will cover his body—soil named after Nemea's flower.

After him, another ruler will rise, an older man with silver hair. His name will have four syllables and be linked to the sea, with the letter A from Ares at the start. He will build temples in many cities and travel the world, bringing back riches like gold and amber. He will rid the sacred places of magicians and replace them with better things for people. While he rules, there will be great peace, and he will be known for his strong voice, fairness, and commitment to justice. But in the end, he will bring about his own downfall.

Following him, three rulers will take the throne, with the third one ruling for three decades. After them, a king from the first unit of numbers will take power, followed by another leader whose number will be seven tens. Their names will be honored, and they will defeat many people, including the Britons, Moors, Dacians, and Arabians.

When the last of these rulers falls, war will break out again. Ares, who was once wounded, will return to battle and destroy the Parthians completely. However, the king himself will be betrayed and killed by a wild beast that was trained by his own hands.

After him, a new ruler will take the throne. He will be wise and skilled in many ways, and his name will be the same as the first great king from the first unit of numbers. He will be strong and do great things for the Latins in memory of his father. He will decorate Rome with gold, silver, and ivory, and walk proudly through the markets and temples with another strong leader.

But soon, terrible wounds of war will spread across Rome. He will launch an attack on the German lands, and during this time, a great sign from God will appear in the sky. God, who sees all, will send unexpected rain when the king prays, protecting soldiers in their bronze armor from destruction.

After these events, as the years pass, this great and righteous king's rule will come to an end. Before he dies, he will name his golden-haired son as his successor. This new ruler, whose name contains two tens, will inherit the kingdom. He will be a brilliant leader, quick-minded, and as strong as the legendary Hercules. He will be a master in battle, hunting, and horseback riding, but he will live a lonely and dangerous life.

During his rule, a terrifying sign will appear: a thick mist will cover Rome's plains so completely that people will be unable to see their neighbors. War and deep sorrow will follow. The king, blinded by his passion, will bring disgrace upon himself by marrying inappropriately and dishonoring his children.

Then, he will face a tragic end—hiding alone, trapped by fate, he will die in a bathhouse, betrayed and defeated by the war god, Ares.

This will be a warning that Rome's downfall is near. Because of its endless hunger for power, many will be killed within the halls of the city. Rome will finally pay for everything it has done, repaying the destruction it once caused in its many wars.

My heart is heavy, and I am filled with sorrow.

From the time Rome's first king gave laws to the people and the Word of God came to earth, until the nineteenth ruler finishes his reign, two hundred and forty-four years will pass. Then, during the rule of the twentieth king, he will be struck down by a sword, spilling blood in the streets of Rome. His name will contain the letter linked to the number eighty, and he will be an old man. Soon, Rome will become a widow, losing its ruler.

During this time, many warriors will rise, bringing battles, bloodshed, and endless suffering. Armies will clash, men and horses will fall in the fields, and war will consume the land.

Another ruler will take power, with the number ten in his name. He will bring pain and hardship, robbing people of their wealth. But his rule will be short-lived, as he will fall in battle, killed by a mighty warrior's sword.

Then, a ruler connected to the number fifty will come from the East. A fierce warrior, he will go to Thrace, only to be driven away. He will flee to Bithynia and the plains of Cilicia, but war will catch up to him, and he will be defeated in Assyria.

After him, a deceitful leader will take control, skilled in trickery and schemes. He will rise from the West, and his name will have the number two hundred. He will start a war for power over the Assyrians, building a massive army and seizing control. He will rule the Romans with force, filled with ruthless ambition. A violent and greedy leader, he will destroy noble families, steal their wealth, and leave the land in ruins. His hunger for power will lead him eastward, spreading deception and chaos wherever he goes.

Then, a young ruler will share power, bearing the name of a great Macedonian leader. He will find himself caught in betrayal and deception, barely escaping a plot against him within his own army. However, the barbaric ruler who seeks to overpower him will meet a sudden death, struck down by a warrior's sword. Even after his death, the people will tear his body apart.

Soon, the kings of Persia will rise, and Roman warriors will battle once again.

Phrygia will suffer from earthquakes, and destruction will come upon Laodicea and Hierapolis. The earth will open, swallowing parts of the cities just as it did once before. The people will mourn as war spreads, and the world will be filled with suffering.

A ruler from the East will march toward Italy, but he will meet his end, falling to the sword. His downfall will be tied to his mother, and he will be remembered with hatred.

The seasons will be unpredictable, shifting in ways people do not understand. Some will suffer while others prosper. But those who honor God and turn away from idolatry will find peace.

Now, Lord of all things, the eternal King, you have placed this prophecy in my heart. I ask you to let me rest now, for I do not fully understand the words I speak. Let this vision end, for my heart is weary from revealing the future of kings and their rise and fall.

Book 13.

The eternal God, who never changes, has commanded me to speak again. He is the one who gives power to kings and takes it away. He decides the length of their rule and when their lives will end.

Even though I do not wish to deliver this message, I must warn kings about what is to come.

War and destruction will spread, led by violent warriors. Many will die—both children and elders who guide their people with wisdom. Battles will rage, bringing hunger, disease, earthquakes, and powerful storms. Armies from Assyria will roam across the land, looting cities and stealing from temples.

A rebellion will rise among the hardworking Persians, joined by the Indians, Armenians, and Arabians. In response, a Roman king, hungry for war, will lead his soldiers into battle against the Assyrians. A young warrior, skilled in combat, will push forward as far as the Euphrates

River. However, he will be betrayed by a trusted friend and fall in battle, struck down by a soldier's sword.

Then, a ruler from Syria, who loves wealth and power, will take control. He will be ruthless in war, and his son will follow in his footsteps, ruling the world with a heavy hand. Both will share the same name, and their combined rule will be marked by the numbers five hundred, one, and twenty. While they are in power, laws will be passed, and there will be a short time of peace. But it will not last.

A deceiver will rise, pretending to make peace with his enemies. Like a wolf promising to protect a flock of sheep, he will take an oath only to break it. He will betray and destroy those who trusted him, throwing away his promises.

Then, war will break out again between proud and greedy kings. Many people will suffer, including the Syrians, Indians, Armenians, Arabians, Persians, and Babylonians. These nations will destroy each other in terrible battles.

When a powerful Roman warrior defeats a fierce German leader, war will continue for many years among the Persians. But they will not find victory. Just as a fish cannot climb a steep mountain, a turtle cannot fly, and an eagle cannot live in the sea, so too will the Persians struggle and fail in battle.

Meanwhile, the land of the Italians, resting near the sacred waters of the Nile, will send aid to the seven-hilled city of Rome. As long as Rome's name remains in the pages of history, the great city built by the Macedonian ruler will provide food to its people.

I will now tell of terrible suffering for the people of Alexandria, who will be destroyed because of the cruelty of wicked rulers. Once-powerful men will become weak and beg for peace as corruption spreads among their leaders.

God's anger will fall upon the Assyrians, and a great flood will wipe them out, reaching even the city of Caesar and harming the people of Canaan.

The Pyramus River will flood the city of Mopsus, and the people of Aegea will fall because of violent conflicts among strong warriors.

Antioch will not escape suffering, as a great war will surround it. A powerful leader will rise within its walls and battle against the Persian archers. He will gain control over Rome and lead its armies.

Cities of Arabia will be filled with grand temples, open markets, and great wealth. Statues of gold, silver, and ivory will be everywhere. Bostra and Philippopolis, known for their love of learning, will later suffer great sorrow.

Even the stars and signs in the sky will not help them. Aries, Taurus, Gemini, and the other constellations will not bring any relief. Those who put their trust in such things will find themselves betrayed.

Now, I will speak of Alexandria's wars. Its people will turn against one another, and many will die as their own city is destroyed. They will fight for power and greed, and the god of war will rage among them. A leader with a strong heart, along with his mighty son, will fall in betrayal because of an older ruler.

After this, another powerful ruler will take over fertile Rome. He will be skilled in war and come from the Dacians. His name will carry the number three hundred, along with the number four. He will kill many people, including his own brothers and close friends, while other kings are slaughtered. Chaos, robbery, and murder will follow because of the older ruler's death.

Then, a cunning man will appear, a thief and a stranger to Rome, coming from Syria. Using deception, he will invade Cappadocia, bringing destruction. Tyana and Mazaka will be conquered, and their people will be enslaved again, forced to carry heavy burdens. Syria will mourn the loss of its people, and even the goddess of the moon will not protect her city.

When this ruler flees from Syria and faces the Romans, he will no longer fight like them but will take on the ways of the Persian archers. Then, fulfilling fate, the ruler of Italy will fall in battle, struck down by a shining sword. Soon after, his children will perish as well.

A new ruler will take control of Rome, but soon, unstable nations will rise against the empire. Rome's walls will be surrounded by war and destruction. Famine, disease, powerful storms, and terrible battles will follow. Cities will fall into chaos, and many Syrians will be wiped out.

God's great wrath will strike them, and the Persians will join the Syrians in attacking the Romans. However, they will not be able to fully conquer the land or destroy its laws.

Many people will flee from the East, seeking safety in foreign lands. The ground will be soaked in the blood of countless victims. It will be a time when the living will envy the dead, and people will see death as a blessing—but death will not come for them.

Now, I mourn for Syria, for a terrible disaster will strike its people. Deadly arrows will rain down upon them from an enemy they never expected.

A fugitive from Rome will arrive, leading a vast army and carrying a great spear. Crossing the Euphrates River with thousands of soldiers, he will burn Syria to the ground and leave it in ruins.

Antioch, your fate is sealed. You will no longer be called a city, for your lack of wisdom will lead to your downfall. Your streets will be filled with enemy soldiers, and your homes will be stripped bare. Left with nothing, you will become an empty shell, abandoned and ruined.

Many will weep suddenly when they see the destruction.

Hierapolis, you will be taken in victory, and so will you, Beroea. Chalcis, you will cry for your sons who have been wounded in battle.

So many will suffer near the steep mountains of Casius and Amanus. So many will be lost near the rivers Lycus, Marsyas, and the silver-flowing Pyramus. The conquerors will take everything from Asia, stealing treasures, leaving cities in ruins, and destroying temples.

One day, sorrow will fall upon the Gauls, Pannonians, Mysians, and Bithynians when a mighty warrior arrives.

Lycians, beware—a fierce enemy, like a wolf, will come to spill your blood. The Sannians will invade, bringing destruction, while the Carpians and Ausonians prepare for war.

A king's illegitimate son will betray him, taking his life through treachery. But he, too, will soon die because of his own wickedness. Another ruler will follow, his name beginning with the first letter, but he will not last long either, falling in battle by a warrior's sword.

The world will fall into chaos once again. People will die from both war and disease. The Persians, angered by the Ausonians, will return to battle, causing the Romans to flee.

A priest, famous everywhere, will rise from Syria, acting with deception to achieve his goals. The city of the sun will pray for protection, while the Persians will threaten the Phoenicians.

When two strong leaders take control of Rome, one with the number seventy and the other with three, chaos will follow. A mighty bull will charge, kicking up dust with its hooves, attacking a dark serpent that slithers on the ground. But in the end, the bull itself will fall.

After him, a swift and hungry stag will roam the mountains, searching for food among dangerous creatures.

Then, a fierce lion will come, sent by the sun, breathing fire. It will destroy the powerful stag and strike down a deadly serpent that makes a terrible hissing sound. The sideways-moving goat will fall as well, and this lion will gain great fame.

The lion will rule over Rome, and the Persians will grow weak.

Lord, ruler of the world, let this song come to an end and bring peace to our words.

Book 14.

O people, why do you dream of things too great, as if you will live forever?

You rule for only a short time, yet you desire power over everyone. You do not understand that God despises greed for power and hates wicked rulers who crave control. Because of this, he sends darkness upon them, and instead of doing what is right, they dress in royal robes and seek war and bloodshed. But God, who is eternal, will shorten their reigns and bring them to ruin, one after another.

Then a fierce leader will rise, strong and wild, destroying everything in his path. He will tear apart even the shepherds, and no one will stop him unless fast and clever young warriors chase him down through the forests. A great battle will come when a brave fighter hunts down the beast that has terrorized the people.

After this, another ruler will take power, a man with a name of four syllables, and his name will begin with the first number. But war will quickly bring him down.

Then two leaders, both connected to the number forty, will rule together. Under them, peace and justice will spread across the land. However, greedy men, hungry for gold and silver, will betray them and take their lives using cunning plans.

After them, a young and fierce ruler, marked by the number seventy, will rise. He will betray Rome's army and cause great suffering. Because of his actions, cities and homes will be destroyed, and Rome will fall. The once-great city will be nothing but ashes, with nothing left of its former glory.

Then, from the sky, God will send fire and destruction. He will strike the wicked with lightning and thunder, burning some and crushing others. The cruel ruler who caused Rome's downfall will be killed by the very people he betrayed. His body will not be buried with honor, but left for the birds and wild beasts to devour.

After him, another leader, known for conquering the Parthians and Germans, will take power. He will hunt and destroy the wild beasts that threaten people along the oceans and the Euphrates River. Under him, Rome will regain its strength.

But soon, a fierce enemy will come, like a wolf invading the land. He will march from the West, but before he can rule for long, he will be struck down by a warrior's sword.

Another great leader, from Assyria, will rise. His name will start with the first letter, and he will try to bring order through war. But treacherous forces will turn against him, and he will fall in battle.

After him, three powerful rulers will come. One will have the first number, another the number thirty, and the last will be connected to three hundred. They will be cruel men who melt gold and silver to create false idols. To win wars, they will use money to bribe armies, giving out treasures and riches.

They will fight against the Parthians, the Medes, and the strong warriors of Persia. When one of them dies, he will leave his kingdom to his sons, hoping they will rule wisely. But instead, they will ignore his words and fight among themselves for power.

Then another ruler, tied to the number three, will take control, but he will not last long before he is struck down by the sword. After him, many will fight and kill one another, each trying to claim the throne.

A strong and wise leader will rule over the powerful Romans. He will be an older man, connected to the number four, and will govern well.

Then, war will come to Phoenicia as Persian archers attack. Many people will fall to these invaders who speak foreign tongues. The cities of Sidon, Tripoli, and Berytus, once proud and strong, will see their streets covered in blood and bodies.

Laodicea will bring upon itself a terrible and hopeless war because of the sins of its people.

The people of Tyre will suffer greatly. In the middle of the day, the sun will disappear, and dark red rain will fall from the sky. During this time, the king will be betrayed by those closest to him. After his death, corrupt leaders will rise, continuing the cycle of violence and killing each other for power.

Then, a wise and respected ruler will take the throne. His name will be tied to the number five, and he will command a strong army. The people will admire him for his leadership, and he will build a good reputation through his actions. But during his reign, a terrible event will occur between the Taurus and Amanus mountains. A new, strong, and beautiful city in Cilicia, near powerful rivers, will be destroyed. Many earthquakes will also shake Propontis and Phrygia. In the end, this great king will die from a deadly illness.

After him, two kings will rule. One will be connected to the number three hundred, and the other to the number three. They will destroy many enemies to defend the seven-hilled city of Rome and maintain their control. But trouble will come to the senate, as the ruling king will hold deep anger against it. A strange sign will appear for all to see, and the world will experience heavy rain, snow, and hail, ruining crops. These kings will ultimately die in wars fought for Italy.

Then, another ruler will rise—a cunning man who will gather a great army. To prepare for war, he will give money to soldiers wearing bronze armor. But during his reign, the Nile River will flood beyond the Libyan lands, bringing water to Egypt for two years. Despite this, famine, war, and crime will spread, leading to the destruction of many cities. In the end, this ruler will be betrayed and killed by the sword.

After him, a leader tied to the number three hundred will take control of Rome and its mighty warriors. He will lead brutal attacks against the Armenians, Parthians, Assyrians, and Persians. During his reign, Rome will be rebuilt with gold, silver, ivory, and amber, making it grander than ever. People from both the East and the West will gather there, and the ruler will create new laws. But in the end, he will meet his fate on a distant island.

Then, another ruler will take power, connected to the number thirty. He will be fierce, wild-haired, and descended from the Greeks. His rule will bring destruction to the cities of Molossian Phthia and Larissa along the Peneus River.

At the same time, an uprising will break out in Scythia, and war will rage near Lake Maeotis and the river Phasis. Many warriors will die in battle. The king will defeat the Scythians, but after his victory, his life will come to an end.

Another ruler, connected to the number four, will take power. He will be a terrifying leader, feared in battle by the Armenians, who drink the cold waters of the Araxes River, and by the strong-willed Persians. War will break out between the Colchians and the mighty Pelasgians. The people of Phrygia and those near the Propontis will also fight, drawing their swords in violent battles driven by wickedness.

Then, with time, God will send a great sign from the sky—a bat, warning of an upcoming war. The king will not escape his fate; he will be struck down by a sword and die.

After him, another ruler, tied to the number fifty, will rise from Asia. He will be a fierce warrior, engaging in hand-to-hand combat. He will bring war to the grand walls of Rome and battle the Colchians, Heniochi, and the nomadic Agathyrsians by the Black Sea and the shores of Thrace. But his end will be brutal—he will be slain, and his body will be torn apart.

With the death of the king, Rome, once great and filled with people, will become a desolate land. Many will perish.

Then, a terrifying ruler will emerge from Egypt. He will defeat the powerful Parthians, Medes, and Germans, along with the Agathyrsians of the Bosporus, the Iernians, the Britons, and the Iberians. He will also fight the Massagetæ, skilled archers, and the Persians, who think themselves invincible.

A renowned leader will rise against all of Greece, treating Scythia and the towering Caucasus Mountains as his enemies.

During his reign, a strange sign will appear—crowns that shine like stars will be seen in the sky over both the northern and southern lands. When he dies, he will pass his power to his son, whose name starts with the first letter of the alphabet. The king will meet his fate and descend into the underworld.

When this son takes control of Rome, his rule—marked by the number one—will bring a long-awaited peace across the world. The Latins will cherish him as their king, remembering the legacy of his father. Though he will long to travel east and west, the Roman people will hold him back, insisting he remain as their ruler. They will feel a deep loyalty to their noble leader.

However, death will come swiftly, taking him too soon. Afterward, chaos will return as powerful warriors fight among themselves, no longer ruling as kings but as cruel tyrants. Across the world, they will bring suffering, especially to the Romans, until the arrival of a third leader named Dionysus.

Then, from Egypt, a warlike ruler will rise, known as Dionysus the Lord. When the royal purple cloak is torn apart by a violent lion and lioness, the kingdom will shift. But a righteous king, whose name begins with the first letter of the alphabet, will rise up. He will crush his enemies, leaving their bodies to be devoured by dogs and birds.

Oh, Rome, once powerful, you will be burned by fire. So much suffering awaits you when these events take place. But later, a great and famous ruler will rebuild you, using gold, silver, amber, and ivory. Once again, you will be rich in temples, marketplaces, and arenas. You will shine like before, a guiding light for all.

But woe to the lands of Cecropes, Cadmeans, and the Spartans—those who live near the Peneus River and the Molossian waters, the cities of Tricca, Dodona, Ithome, and the peaks of Olympus, Ossa, Larissa, and Calydon.

A great sign will appear—a darkened day like twilight covering the earth. This will mark the end for a powerful king, who will be struck down by his own brother's arrow. Afterward, another ruler will rise, a fiery leader from a royal bloodline. He will seize power over Egypt's people. Though younger than his brother, he will be much stronger. His name will be linked to the number eighty.

Then, the whole world will face the unstoppable anger of God. Humanity will suffer from famine, plagues, war, and endless violence. Darkness will cover the earth, bringing destruction. From the sky, storms, hail, and fiery thunderbolts will strike, while the ground shakes beneath Scythian hills and Greek cities. Many places will crumble under God's wrath, set ablaze by burning lightning.

The great ruler will not escape fate—his own men will kill him as if he were nothing. After him, many men from the Latin people will wear the purple robe of power. They will fight for control, each one eager to rule.

Three kings will rise in Rome, two connected to the first number, and one with a name meaning victory. They will love Rome and the world, hoping to bring peace to its people. But they will fail because God will not be merciful. Humanity has done too much evil, and punishment will continue.

God will allow cruel leaders to take control—men even more vicious than wolves or leopards. They will be ruthless, betraying and killing kings like helpless victims. Rome's great leaders, believing in false promises, will be destroyed.

Warriors, chaotic and full of rage, will attack without order. They will spill the blood of noble families and first-born sons, bringing Rome to ruin. Three times, the Most High will bring terrible judgment upon the world, destroying both people and their wicked works. But those with shameless hearts, who have committed evil, will still be judged. They will be trapped, falling upon one another, and condemned for their wickedness.

A bright comet will signal what is to come—war, destruction, and great battles.

During these troubled times, a leader will collect prophecies from distant lands, predicting disaster for temples and cities. He will order Rome to store up wheat and barley for twelve months, preparing for hardship. The city will suffer greatly, but then it will recover. Peace will return only when this ruler is gone.

After that, the final race of Latin kings will rule. But after them, a new kingdom will rise, strong and unshaken. It will be clear to all that God himself is the true king.

There is a special land, rich and fertile, lying in a great plain. The Nile River surrounds it, separating it from Libya and Ethiopia.

The Syrians, scattered from different places, will take everything they can carry. A strong and wise ruler will take charge, training young men and sending soldiers to battle. He will focus on a terrifying war and send a powerful ally to help all of Italy. When he reaches the dark sea near Assyria, he will attack the Phoenicians in their homes, bringing destruction and fierce battles. He will rule as one of the two most powerful leaders on earth.

Now I must speak of the terrible fate awaiting Alexandria. Foreign invaders will take over Egypt, a land that once stood strong and untouched. When the gods' anger falls upon it, there will be great suffering.

A great change will come, making winter feel like summer. Prophecies will be fulfilled. When three young men win at the Olympian games, they will be asked to perform a cleansing ritual using the blood of a newborn animal. But this will not stop what is coming. Three times, the Most High will bring disaster. A heavy spear will be raised over all people, and blood will flood the ground when a city is completely destroyed by cruel invaders.

Blessed are those who are already dead, and even more blessed are those without children. The leader, once known for his freedom, will abandon his past ideals and force his people into slavery. A new ruler will bring great sorrow. Soon, a doomed army of Sicilians will arrive, bringing even more destruction. Another foreign army will strike, cutting down crops before they can be harvested. The great thunderous God will punish them, and people will fight over stolen gold, taking it from one another.

When people witness the fall of the powerful lion, a deadly lioness will follow, bringing even more destruction. The ruler's power will be stripped away. Just as people in Egypt celebrate feasts and cheer loudly, so too will the world be filled with the noise of war, terror, and destruction. Many will die, and people will turn against each other in brutal battles.

Then a figure covered in dark scales will rise, joined by two others working together. A third leader, a great warrior from Cyrene, once a refugee in Egypt, will also rise. However, none of their plans will succeed.

For a time, the world will be peaceful, but another war will soon break out in Egypt. A great naval battle will take place, but the victors will not hold onto their power for long. A famous city will be conquered, but only briefly.

People from neighboring lands will flee, leading their families to safety. But when they return, they will fight for victory. The Jews, strong warriors, will battle fiercely to protect their homeland and loved ones. Great warriors will be counted among the dead. Many will drown in the sea, and the shores will be covered in bodies. Birds will feast on golden-haired soldiers who have fallen in battle.

Arabian lands will be soaked in blood. When wolves and dogs

swear false oaths on an island, a great tower will be built. A once-ruined city will be inhabited again. Gold and silver will lose their value, and people will no longer fight over wealth. Servitude will end. People will live together in friendship, sharing everything equally. Evil will vanish from the world, sinking deep into the sea.

The time of judgment for humanity will arrive. These events must happen. But even in those days, no traveler will say that humanity is coming to an end. A holy nation will rise and rule the world forever, with strong and noble leaders guiding them.

The Vision of Ezra

Introduction

The Vision of Ezra is an ancient text that describes what happens after death, showing the rewards of the righteous and the punishments of the wicked. It is written as a series of visions experienced by Ezra, also known as Salathiel.

Although the text claims that Ezra wrote it, scholars believe it was actually written sometime between the 2nd and 10th centuries AD. The oldest copies that still exist today are in Latin and date back to the 11th century. However, experts think the original text was written in Greek, suggesting it came from a Hellenistic background. The exact time it was written is unknown, but its style and themes are similar to Christian writings from the 3rd and 4th centuries.

The Vision of Ezra has been found in seven Latin manuscripts from the 11th to the 13th centuries, with important copies stored in the Vatican Library and other monasteries in Austria. The similarities between these copies show that the text was well-known and influential in medieval Christian teachings.

The story follows Ezra on a deep spiritual journey. He asks for the strength to witness God's judgment on sinners, and in response, seven angels guide him through the different levels of punishment. Along the way, he sees:

- Fiery Gates – These are guarded by lions that breathe flames.

- Punishment of Sinners – The wicked suffer in terrifying ways, such as being attacked by wild dogs or burned in fire.

• Reward of the Righteous – Those who have lived well pass safely through fire, which purifies them and prepares them for salvation.

These powerful images highlight the difference between the fate of good and evil people, showing God's justice and mercy.

The Vision of Ezra reflects early Christian beliefs about the afterlife and final judgment. It describes heaven and hell in great detail, offering lessons on morality, repentance, and salvation. The text also emphasizes free will, showing that people's choices in life determine what happens to them after death.

This text has similarities to other apocalyptic writings, such as the Greek Apocalypse of Ezra and 2 Esdras (also called 4 Ezra). All of these focus on visions of the afterlife and divine judgment, but the Vision of Ezra is shorter and tells a more focused story. Its unique feature is Ezra's journey through different spiritual realms, guided by angels.

The Vision of Ezra gives a strong picture of early Christian beliefs about what happens after death, God's judgment, and the choices people make in life. Its detailed descriptions and important lessons still have meaning today, offering a glimpse into the religious and spiritual ideas of the past.

The Book of Ezra the Scribe, Who Is Called Salathiel

Vision I

Introduction (III. I 3).

In the 30th year after our city was destroyed, I, Salathiel, also known as Ezra, was in Babylon. I lay on my bed, feeling troubled, as many thoughts filled my mind. I saw how Zion had been left in ruins while

Babylon's homes were filled with riches. My heart was overwhelmed, and I cried out to God in fear.

I said, "Lord, didn't you speak from the beginning when you created the earth? You alone shaped everything, commanding the dust to form Adam. You breathed life into him, and he became a living being. You placed him in the paradise you had prepared before the earth existed.

You gave him one command, but he disobeyed it. Because of this, you sentenced him and his descendants to death. From him came many nations, tribes, and languages—too many to count. They all followed their own ways, committing evil, but you did not stop them.

Then, in time, you sent a great flood to destroy the people of the world because of their wickedness. They all perished, just as Adam faced death. But you spared one man and his family, and from them, all the righteous people were born.

As people multiplied again, their wickedness grew worse than before. When they turned away from you, you chose one man, Abraham. You loved him and revealed your plans for the future. You made an everlasting covenant with him, promising to never abandon his descendants.

You gave him Isaac, and to Isaac, you gave Jacob and Esau. You chose Jacob's descendants as your own people, while you rejected Esau. Jacob's family grew into a great nation. When you brought them out of Egypt, you renewed your covenant with them and led them to Mount Sinai.

You shook the heavens and the earth, causing the sea to tremble and the world to fear your power. Your glory passed through fire, earthquakes, wind, and cold to give Jacob's descendants your Law and commandments. But even then, you did not remove their sinful hearts.

Because of Adam, sin had taken root, and everyone born after him inherited his weakness. Even with your Law, people still chose evil.

As time passed, you raised up a servant, David, and commanded him to build a city for your name, a place where offerings would be made to you. For many years, this was done. But the people of that city also sinned against you, just as Adam and his descendants had done. They followed their sinful hearts, so you allowed their enemies to take the city.

Seeing this, I wondered in my heart: Are the people of Babylon really better? Have you abandoned Zion for them? Since I arrived here, I have witnessed endless sins. For 30 years, I have seen terrible wrongdoing. My heart is troubled because I see you allow sinners to thrive, while your own people have been destroyed, and your enemies remain untouched.

You have not made it clear how anyone can understand your ways. Has Babylon really done better than Zion? Is there any other nation you favor more than Israel? What other people have kept your covenant like Jacob's descendants? Yet, they have not been rewarded, and their hard work has not paid off.

I have traveled among many nations and seen that they are successful, even though they do not follow your commands. If you weigh our sins against those of the rest of the world, the balance would not tip much in either direction. Have the people of the world ever stopped sinning before you? Has any nation truly obeyed your laws? There may be a few individuals who have followed your commands, but not an entire people.

Then the angel Uriel, who had been sent to me, spoke and said, "Are you so troubled by this world that you wish to understand the ways of the Most High?"

I replied, "Yes, my Lord."

The angel continued, "I have three challenges for you. If you can answer one of them, I will show you the truth about why there is evil in the world."

I said, "Please tell me."

He said, "Weigh fire on a scale, measure the wind, or bring back a day that has already passed."

I answered, "No one born of man could do these things. Why do you ask me something impossible?"

Then he said, "What if I had asked you how many chambers are in the ocean, how many springs flow from underground, or how many paths lead to heaven? Could you answer? You would say you have never gone to the depths of the sea, nor to the underworld, nor have you risen to heaven. But I did not ask about those things. I asked about fire, wind, and time—things you live with every day. And yet, you cannot explain them."

Then he said, "If you cannot understand what happens around you, how can you expect to understand the ways of the Most High? His ways are beyond human understanding. A mortal person living in a corrupt world cannot grasp the wisdom of an eternal God."

When I heard this, I fell to the ground and said, "It would have been better if we had never been born. Now we live in sin, we suffer, and we do not even understand why."

The angel answered, "Let me tell you a story.

"Once, the trees of the forest gathered together and said, 'Let's go to war against the sea so that it will move back and give us more land to grow.'

"But the waves of the sea also gathered together and said, 'Let's go to war against the trees so that we can take their land for the waters.'

"But in the end, fire came and burned the trees, and the sand rose up to stop the waves. Both plans were useless.

"If you had been the judge, who would you say was right and who was wrong?"

I replied, "Neither plan made sense. The trees were meant to stay on the land, and the sea was meant to hold its waves."

Then the angel said, "You have judged correctly! So why do you not judge yourself in the same way? Just as trees belong to the land and waves belong to the sea, people on earth can only understand what happens on earth. Only those in heaven can understand the things above."

I answered, "Then tell me, my Lord, why was I given the ability to think if I cannot understand these things? I am not asking about what is above the heavens. I only want to understand what happens around me every day.

"Why has Israel been handed over to other nations? Why have your chosen people fallen into the hands of those who do not believe in you? Why has the holy Law been ignored? Why have the covenants written for us disappeared?

"We pass from this world like insects, and our lives are as brief as a breath. We do not deserve your mercy, but what will you do for the sake of your great name, which we carry? That is what I want to understand."

The Answer

The angel answered me, "If you live long enough, you will see and be amazed because this world is quickly passing away. It cannot last forever, especially since it is full of suffering and pain. It is not strong enough to hold the great rewards promised to the righteous.

"The evil you asked me about has already been planted, but its time to be harvested has not yet come. Until the evil is removed, the good cannot fully grow. From the very beginning, one seed of evil was planted in Adam's heart, and look at how much sin it has produced over time. And it will continue until the time for the harvest arrives.

"Now, think for yourself—how much wickedness has grown from that one seed? So imagine when countless seeds of goodness are planted—how great will the harvest be?"

I asked, "How long will it take for this to happen? Our lives are short and full of trouble."

The angel replied, "You cannot rush ahead of the Most High. You want things to happen quickly for yourself, but God is waiting for the sake of many. Even the souls of the righteous, who are waiting in their resting places, ask, 'How much longer must we wait? When will we receive our reward?'

"The angel Remiel answered them, saying, 'You must wait until the full number of righteous people has been reached.'

"The Holy One has measured the world carefully. He has counted the times and set the seasons in place. He will not change anything or rush the process until everything is complete."

I said, "Lord, but the world is full of sin! Are the righteous being delayed because of all the evil that people do?"

The angel answered, "Go ask a pregnant woman if she can hold her baby inside her after nine months."

I replied, "No, my Lord, she cannot."

Then he said, "The underworld and the resting places of souls are like a mother's womb. Just as a woman cannot hold back her child when it is time to give birth, the world cannot delay what has been set in motion. When the time comes, everything that has been waiting since the beginning will be revealed."

I asked, "If I have found favor in your eyes, please show me something else. Has more time already passed than what remains? I know about the past, but I do not know what is still ahead."

The angel said, "Stand to my right, and I will show you."

I stood and saw a huge fire burning fiercely. When the flames died down, I saw that smoke remained. Then I saw a heavy storm cloud filled with water, pouring down a violent rain. But after the storm passed, a few drops of water were still left behind.

Then the angel said, "Think about what you saw. Just as the fire was much greater than the smoke, and the rain was heavier than the drops that remained, so too has most of time already passed. Only a little remains."

The Signs Which Precede the End
(IV. 51-V.13)

I asked him, "Will I live to see those days? Who will be alive when these things happen?"

He answered, "I can tell you some of the signs you asked about, but I was not sent to tell you about your life. I do not know the answer to that."

"As for the signs," he continued, "the time is coming when people on earth will be overcome with fear. Truth will be hidden, and faith will disappear. Sin and shamelessness will be worse than anything you see now or have heard about in the past.

"The land you see now will become unstable and abandoned. If the Most High allows you to live, you will see the land in total confusion after three days.

"Strange things will happen. The sun will shine at night, and the moon will be bright during the day. Trees will drip blood, and stones will speak. People will be in chaos, and the air will change.

"A ruler will rise whom no one expects, and birds will leave their usual places.

"The sea of Sodom will be full of fish, and a mysterious voice will be heard at night, surprising everyone.

"Cracks will open in many places, and fire will keep bursting out. Wild animals will leave their habitats, and strange things will happen to pregnant women—some babies will not develop fully before birth.

"Fresh water will become salty. Friends will suddenly turn against each other in battle.

"Wisdom will disappear, and understanding will be hidden. People will search for them but will not find them.

"Sin and shamelessness will spread everywhere. People will ask their neighbors, 'Have you seen anyone doing what is right?' But the answer will always be 'No.'

"During that time, people will hope but never receive what they wish for. The land will struggle to produce food, and hard work will not lead to success.

"I was told to share these signs with you. But if you pray again as you have been doing, and fast for seven more days, you will hear even greater things."

The Conclusion of The Vision
(V. 14-19)

I woke up, shaking all over, and felt so weak that it seemed like my life was slipping away.

But the angel who had been speaking to me reached out, helped me stand, and gave me strength.

On the second night, Phaltiel, the leader of the people, came to me and asked, "Where have you been? Why do you look so troubled? Don't you know that you have been chosen to care for Israel while they are in captivity?

"Get up and eat something so you don't abandon us, like a shepherd leaving his flock to be attacked by wolves!"

But I told him, "Leave me alone. Do not come near me for seven days. After that, you can return, and I will explain everything to you."

After I said this, he left.

Vision II

The Prayer of Ezra 1

I fasted for seven days, crying and mourning, just as the angel Ramiel had told me to do. After the seven days, my heart was still troubled, and I felt overwhelmed with thoughts. But then, my soul was filled with understanding, and I began to pray again, speaking to the Most High with deep pleading.

I said, "Lord, from all the trees in the world, you have chosen one vine. From all the lands, you have picked one special place. From the deep waters of the sea, you have set aside one river. Among all the flowers, you have chosen one. From all the cities ever built, you made Zion your holy place.

"Among all the birds, you have named one dove as special. From all the animals, you have chosen one sheep. And from all the nations, you have brought one people close to you, giving them the law you approved of and loved.

"But now, Lord, why have you given the chosen one over to so many? Why have you allowed your special people to be scattered among the nations? Those who reject your commandments have trampled on the ones who believed in your covenant. If you were so angry with your people, shouldn't you have punished them yourself instead of letting others destroy them?"

After I finished speaking, the angel who had appeared to me before returned and said, "Listen to me, Ezra, and I will explain. Look at me, and I will give you understanding."

I replied, "Speak, my lord."

The angel asked, "Are you so troubled about Israel? Do you love them more than the One who created them?"

I said, "No, my lord! But my heart is in pain, and I suffer every moment because I want to understand God's judgment."

The angel said, "You cannot understand."

I asked, "Why not, my lord? Why was I even born if I cannot understand these things? Why wasn't my mother's womb my grave so I would not have to see the suffering of Jacob and the pain of Israel's descendants?"

The angel answered, "If you can count the people who have not yet been born, gather the raindrops that have fallen, or make dead flowers bloom again—if you can open doors that have never been unlocked, control the winds that are held back, or show me the face of someone you have never seen—then I will tell you what you want to know."

I replied, "Lord, only the One who does not live among men can know these things. I am weak and foolish—how could I possibly understand what you ask?"

The angel said, "Just as you cannot do any of these things, you also cannot understand God's judgment or the depth of the love He has promised His people."

Then I asked, "Lord, you made promises to those who will live at the end of time. But what about the people who came before us, those who live now, and those who will come after us?"

The angel answered, "God's judgment is fair to all. There is no advantage for those who came first, and no disadvantage for those who come last."

I asked, "But couldn't you have created everyone all at once so that we could all be judged together?"

The angel answered me and said, "Creation does not move faster than its Creator. If everything were created all at once, the world would not be able to support it."

I replied, "But you just told me that all creation will be brought back to life at the same time. If that is true, then why couldn't everything have been made at once from the start?"

The angel responded, "Ask a woman who is pregnant, 'If you carry ten children, why don't you give birth to them all at once?' Demand that she deliver them all at the same time."

I answered, "She cannot, my lord. She can only give birth at the right time."

He said, "In the same way, I have made the earth like a womb, where people come into the world at different times. Just as a newborn child cannot give birth and an old woman can no longer bear children, I have set the world in order."

Then I asked, "Since you have explained this to me, let me ask another question. The city of Zion, which you spoke about—does she still have her strength, or is she growing old?"

The angel said, "Ask a mother who has given birth, and she will tell you. Say to her, 'Why are the children you bear now smaller than those who came before?' She will answer, 'Children born when I was young were strong, but those born when I was old are weaker because my body has aged.'

"In the same way, if you look at the people of today, you will see that they are smaller and weaker than those who lived before them. And the people who come after you will be even weaker because creation itself is growing old, and its strength is fading."

Then I said, "Please, my lord, if I have found favor in your eyes, tell me who will bring the end of the world."

The angel answered, "The beginning was in the hands of men, but the end will come by my own hands.

"Before the land of the world was formed, before the winds blew, before thunder was heard, before lightning flashed, before the garden of Paradise was planted, before the flowers bloomed, before the mighty forces of nature moved, before the angels gathered, before the sky stretched high, before the foundations of Zion were set, before the present time was measured, before people began to sin, and before those with faith were chosen—I had already planned it all. Everything that exists was made by my own hand, not by anyone else."

Then I asked, "What does it mean that time will be divided? When will the first age end and the next one begin?"

The angel answered, "From Abraham to Abraham. Abraham had Isaac, and Isaac had Jacob and Esau. When they were born, Jacob held Esau's heel.

"Esau represents the end of one time, and Jacob represents the beginning of another. Just as a man's life starts with his hand and ends with his heel, time moves in the same way. There is nothing more you need to understand, Ezra."

The Signs of The Last Time and The End

I replied, "Lord, if I have found favor in your eyes, please show me the full meaning of the signs you have revealed to me in part during the night."

The angel answered, "Stand up on your feet, and you will hear a loud voice. If the ground beneath you shakes while you listen, do not be afraid. The voice will be speaking about the end of time, and even the foundations of the earth will understand this message. They will shake and tremble because they will know that their time is changing."

As I listened, I stood up and heard a voice like the sound of rushing waters. It said:

"The time is coming when I will visit those who live on the earth and hold the wicked accountable for their actions. When the suffering of Zion is finished and this world is about to come to an end, I will show these signs:

- The books of judgment will be opened in the sky, and everyone will see my decision.

- One-year-old children will be able to speak.

- Pregnant women will give birth after only three or four months, and their babies will live and move.

- Fields that were once empty will suddenly grow crops.

- Storehouses full of food will suddenly be empty.

- A loud trumpet will sound, and everyone will hear it and be afraid.

- Friends will turn against each other like enemies, and the earth will be shocked by what happens.

- Springs of water will stop flowing for three hours.

Anyone who survives these events will witness my salvation and the end of the world. They will see those who have been taken up and have never experienced death. The hearts and minds of the people will be changed, and they will think differently.

- Evil will be wiped away, and lies will disappear.

- Faith will grow, and corruption will be defeated.

- Truth will finally appear after being hidden for so many years."

As the voice spoke, I felt the ground beneath me begin to shake little by little.

The Conclusion of The Vision
(VI. 30-34)

The angel said to me, "I have come to reveal these things to you tonight. If you pray and fast for another seven days, I will show you even greater things.

Your voice has been heard by the Most High. The Mighty One has seen your sincerity and the holiness you have shown since your youth. That is why He has sent me to reveal these things to you.

Take courage and do not be afraid! But do not be quick to judge the past, or you may be judged in the final days."

Vision III

(VI. . 35-IX. 25)

Introduction (VI. 35-37)

After this, I cried and went without food for seven days so I could complete the three weeks I had been told to do. On the eighth night, I felt troubled again, and I spoke to the Most High because my heart was heavy with emotion, and my soul felt like it was burning inside me.

I said, "Lord, you spoke at the beginning of creation and commanded the heavens and earth to exist, and your Word completed the work. Your Spirit moved over everything, while darkness covered all, and no human voice had yet been heard. Then you commanded a ray of light to come from your treasures so that all your works could be seen.

On the second day, you created the sky to separate the waters, placing some above and some below. On the third day, you gathered the waters into one area, revealing dry land. You set aside part of the land to be used for farming and ordered it to produce food. Immediately, all kinds of fruit grew—too many to count—each with its own taste. Beautiful flowers bloomed in many shapes, and trees appeared, each different from the other. Their scents were beyond description. All of this happened on the third day.

On the fourth day, you commanded the sun, moon, and stars to shine and serve mankind, whom you were about to create. On the fifth day, you told the waters to bring forth all kinds of creatures—birds, fish, and animals—so that they would show your wonders. Though the waters had no life of their own, they produced living things. You also created two great creatures: one you called Behemoth, and the other Leviathan. You separated them because the sea could not hold them both together. Behemoth was placed in a dry area with a thousand mountains, while Leviathan was kept in the waters. You have saved them for when you decide they will be used as food.

On the sixth day, you commanded the earth to bring forth land animals, crawling creatures, and livestock. Over all of these, you placed Adam as their ruler, and from him, we, your chosen people, have come.

I have told you all of this, Lord, because you said you created the world for our sake. But as for the other people who also come from Adam, you said they are nothing, like a drop of water from a bucket or spit on the ground. And yet now, these same people rule over us and oppress us! But we, your chosen people, your firstborn and beloved ones, have been given into their hands.

If this world was created for us, then why do we not rule over it? How much longer must we endure this?"

After I finished speaking, the angel who had visited me before came again and said, "Stand up, Ezra, and listen to the words I have come to tell you."

I said, "Speak, my Lord."

He answered, "Imagine a vast sea that is wide and endless, but there is only a narrow entrance, like a river. If someone wants to enter the sea, see it, and take control of it, they must first go through the narrow path. If they do not pass through the narrow way, how can they ever reach the open sea?"

Listen to this example: There is a city built in a wide valley, filled with many good things. However, the entrance to the city is narrow and placed on high ground. On one side, there is fire, and on the other, deep waters.

A single narrow path runs between them, just wide enough for one person to walk at a time. If someone is meant to inherit that city, how can they receive it unless they first pass through the dangers that block the way?

I answered, "That makes sense, my Lord!" And he said to me, "This is also true for Israel. I created the world for them, but when Adam disobeyed my commands, everything was cursed. That is why life in this world is now full of suffering, pain, and danger. But the next world will be wide, peaceful, and full of everlasting goodness.

If people don't go through struggles and hardships, they won't be able to receive what has been prepared for them.

So why are you upset that people are weak and mortal? Why do you focus only on what is happening now instead of looking at what is to come?

I answered, "Lord, you said in your Law that good people will inherit these blessings, but the wicked will be destroyed. The righteous endure hardships because they hope for a greater reward, but the wicked suffer too—and they never get to see the reward!"

He replied, "You are not wiser than God or greater than the Most High! Many will perish because they rejected my Law, which I gave them so they could live. I told them what to do to avoid punishment, but they refused to listen. Instead, they chose to follow empty and worthless thoughts, turned away from the truth, and even denied that the Most High exists.

They rejected his Law, broke his promises, ignored his commands, and refused to acknowledge his works.

So, Ezra, empty things belong to those who are empty, but those who are full will receive what is full."

The Temporary Messianic Kingdom and The End of The World (VP. 26-[44])

The time is coming when the signs I told you about will happen. The bride, who has been hidden, will appear like a great city, and what was once cut off will be seen again.

Anyone who survives these troubles will witness my wonders.

My son, the Messiah, will be revealed, along with those who are with him, and they will bring joy to those who remain for thirty years. After that time, my son, the Messiah, will die, along with all people who are still living. Then, for seven days, the world will return to the silence it had in the beginning, and no one will be left.

After those seven days, the world will wake up again, and corruption will be destroyed. The earth will give up the dead, the dust will release those buried in it, and the hidden places will return the souls that were placed there. The Most High will sit on the throne of judgment, and the end will come. Mercy will be no more, and patience will be gone. Only my judgment will remain. Truth will stand, and faith will grow.

The good and evil deeds of all people will be revealed. The spirit of torment will appear, but so will the place of rest. The fires of

Gehenna will be shown, but across from it will be the paradise of peace.

Then the Most High will say to the nations, "Look at what you have rejected! See the one you refused to serve and the commands you ignored! Look before you—on one side, rest and joy; on the other, fire and suffering!" That is how he will speak on the Day of Judgment.

On that day, the sun, moon, and stars will not shine. There will be no clouds, lightning, or thunder. The wind, water, and air will not move. There will be no darkness, no morning or evening, no summer or winter. There will be no heat, cold, frost, hail, dew, or rain. Time itself—day and night—will no longer exist. There will be no lamps, no torches, no light, except for the shining glory of the Most High. From that light, people will see what has been decided for them.

There will be a waiting period, like a week of years, but this is part of the plan. I have revealed it only to you.

I answered and said, "Lord, I have said before and I say again: Blessed are those who have lived and obeyed your commands. But what about those I prayed for? Is there anyone who has lived without sin? Is there anyone born who has never disobeyed your command?

Now I see that few will find joy in the world to come, but many will face suffering.

For inside us is an evil heart that leads us away from the right path. It drags us into corruption and shows us the way to death. It leads us far from life, and this has happened not just to a few, but to nearly everyone who has ever lived."

The angel answered me and said, "Listen, Ezra, and I will explain things to you again.

The Most High did not create just one world, but two. You asked why there are so few righteous people, so let me give you an example.

If you had a few precious stones, would you compare them to piles of lead and clay?

I asked, "How does that make sense, Lord?"

And he replied, "Ask the earth, and she will tell you. Speak to her, and she will explain. The earth produces gold, silver, copper, iron, lead, and clay. But silver is more common than gold, copper is more common than silver, iron is more common than copper, lead is more common than iron, and clay is the most common of all. Now, tell me, what is more valuable—the rare things or the abundant ones?"

I answered, "Lord, the things that are rare are the most precious, while the things that are common have little value."

Then he said to me, "Now think about what you just said. People rejoice more over a small amount of something valuable than over an abundance of something worthless. The same is true for my judgment. I take joy in the few who live righteously because they bring glory to my name. But I do not grieve over the many who perish, because they are like a breath of air, like smoke that vanishes, like a flame that burns out and disappears."

Then I cried out, "Oh, earth, what have you done? You have brought forth people who are now doomed to destruction! If human intelligence comes from the dust like everything else, then it would have been better if the dust had never existed, so that intelligence would never have been born.

But now, intelligence grows within us, and that is why we suffer—because we understand what is happening, yet we still perish!

Let the human race mourn, but let the animals of the field rejoice! Let all who are born weep, but let the cattle and sheep celebrate! It is better for them than for us, because they do not fear judgment, they do not know punishment, and they were never promised life after death.

So what good is it for us to live, only to suffer?

Every person is born into sin, burdened with wrongdoing from the start. If we did not have to face judgment after death, it would be better for us!"

Then the angel answered me and said, "When the Most High created the world, Adam, and all who came after him, he also prepared judgment and everything that comes with it.

Now think about your own words—you said that intelligence grows within people. That is exactly why they must face judgment! They had understanding, yet they chose to do evil. They received commandments but did not follow them. The Law was given to them, but they rejected it.

What will they say on the day of judgment? How will they defend themselves when the time comes?

For so long, the Most High has been patient with the people of this world—not for their sake, but because the right time had to come."

The State of The Soul Between Death And Judgement VII.

I asked, "Lord, if I have found favor with you, please tell me this: After we die and our souls leave our bodies, do we rest until the time comes when you renew the world, or do we immediately face torment?"

He answered, "I will explain this to you, but do not associate yourself with those who rebel or suffer punishment. You have stored up good deeds with the Most High, and your reward will be revealed at the appointed time.

As for death, here is what happens: When a person's time to die comes, as determined by the Most High, their spirit leaves their body and returns to the One who gave it. First, the soul acknowledges the glory of God.

But if the soul belonged to someone who denied God, rejected His ways, or hated those who feared Him, it does not enter a place of rest. Instead, it immediately suffers torment in seven ways:

1. They realize they have disobeyed the law of the Most High.

2. They understand they can no longer repent or do good deeds to save themselves.

3. They see the reward given to those who were faithful.

4. They recognize the punishment waiting for them in the end and regret not following God when they had the chance.

5. They look upon the peaceful rest of the righteous souls, knowing they will never experience it.

6. They see the suffering prepared for them and know it is unavoidable.

7. Worst of all, they are consumed with shame and fear as they see the glory of the Most High, the one they disobeyed in life, and they know they will face His judgment.

But for those who have followed the ways of the Most High, this is what happens when their time comes:

While they were alive, they faithfully served God, enduring struggles and hardships to keep His commandments. Because of this, when they die, they experience seven great joys:

1. They rejoice in the victory of overcoming evil desires and staying on the path of life.

2. They see the suffering of the wicked and realize they have been saved from it.

3. They hear the Most High Himself testify that they have been faithful to His law.

4. They rest peacefully in the chambers of the righteous, guarded by angels, and they see the glorious future that awaits them.

5. They celebrate their escape from the struggles of the world, knowing they now inherit an eternal reward.

6. They see how their faces will shine like the sun and how they will become like the stars, never again to experience corruption.

7. Above all, they feel fearless and confident as they prepare to stand before the One they served in life, knowing they will be honored and rewarded by Him.

These are the paths of the righteous after death, but the disobedient will only know suffering. Their souls do not enter a place of peace but remain in torment, grieving and regretting their choices in seven ways.

Then I asked, "After the soul leaves the body, is there a time when it sees these things you have described?"

He answered me, saying, "For seven days after death, souls are free to see these things I have told you about. After that, they are gathered into their resting places."

Then I asked, "If I have found favor with you, please tell me—on the Day of Judgment, will the righteous be able to pray for the wicked or ask the Most High to have mercy on them? Can fathers pray for their sons, or sons for their fathers? Can brothers, relatives, or friends plead for one another?"

He replied, "Since you have been shown favor, I will explain this as well. The Day of Judgment is final and will reveal the truth to all. Just as no one can take another's sickness, hunger, or suffering in their place—whether a father, a son, a master, or a friend—so too, on that day, no one can pray for another. Each person will carry the weight of their own righteousness or sin."

I said, "But Lord, in the past, Abraham prayed for the people of Sodom. Moses prayed for our ancestors in the wilderness when they sinned. Joshua prayed for Israel after Achan's wrongdoing. Samuel prayed in the time of Saul, and David for the suffering of the people. Solomon prayed for those in the Temple. Elijah prayed for rain and even for the dead to come back to life. Hezekiah prayed for the people when Sennacherib attacked. Many have prayed for others before—so why can't this happen on the Day of Judgment?"

He answered, "This world has an end, and God's glory does not remain in it forever. That is why the strong have prayed for the weak. But the Day of Judgment is different. It is the end of this world and the beginning of the next, which will never die. In that world, corruption will be gone, wickedness will be destroyed, and faithlessness will be no more. Righteousness will flourish, and truth will shine. On that day, no one will be able to help those who are condemned, just as no one can harm those who are saved."

The Promises of Future Felicity Only Mock A Sin-Stained Race (VII. [N6]-[131])

I answered, "This is my final thought: It would have been better if the earth had never created Adam, or if, when he was created, you had taught him not to sin.

"What good has it done for people to live in suffering, only to die and face punishment? Oh, Adam, what have you done? You were the one who sinned, but the consequences were not just yours—they became ours too, because we came from you!

"What is the point of being promised eternal life when our actions lead to death? What good is it to be given hope that never fades, when we are trapped in misery? What benefit is there in knowing that places of safety and healing exist if we have lived wickedly?

"We are told that the glory of the Most High will protect those who lived righteously, but we chose to follow evil instead. Paradise, filled with fruit that never withers, joy, and healing, has been revealed, but we cannot enter it because of our sinful ways. The faces of the holy will shine brighter than the stars, but our faces will be covered in darkness.

"When we were alive and doing wrong, we never stopped to think about the suffering we would face after death."

He answered me, saying, "This is the challenge that every person faces in life. If they fail, they will suffer, just as you have said. But if they overcome it, they will receive the rewards I have described.

"This is the same message that Moses gave to the people while he was alive. He told them, 'I have set before you today life and death, good and evil. Choose life, so that you and your children may live.'

"But they refused to listen to him. They ignored the prophets who came after him. And even now, they do not believe what I am telling them.

"So, there should be no sadness over their destruction, just as there is joy over those who have chosen life."

Will The Merciful and Compassionate One Suffer So Many To Perish? (VII. [132.]-VIII. 3)

I answered and said, "Lord, I understand that the Most High is called compassionate because he shows kindness even to those who have not yet been born.

"He is called gracious because he welcomes those who turn to his law.

"He is patient because he gives us, his creation, time even when we sin.

"He is generous because he prefers to give rather than take.

"He is full of mercy because he offers kindness not just to those who are alive now, but also to those who have passed and those who are yet to come.

"If he did not show such great mercy, neither the world nor its people would be able to survive.

"He is generous because, in his goodness, he lessens the punishment of sinners—otherwise, hardly one in ten thousand people would still be alive.

"He is also a judge, because if he did not forgive those he created and overlook many of their sins, only a very small number of people would remain."

VIII. R. And He Answered and Said to Me: This World Hath the Most High Made for The Sake of Many, But That Which Is to Come for The Sake of Few.

I will share a parable with you, Ezra. If you ask the earth what it produces more of—ordinary clay or precious gold—it will tell you that common dust is far more abundant than gold. The same is true for this world: many people are created, but only a few truly live.

I answered and said, "Let my soul seek understanding, and let my heart gain wisdom! We come into this world without choosing to, and we leave it without wanting to. We are only given a short time to live.

Lord, if you allow me, I will pray to you. Please give us new hearts that can grow good and lasting things so that those who are weak and temporary can have life.

You are the one and only Creator, and we are the work of your hands, as you have said. In the womb, you form our bodies and shape our features. You protect us in warmth and water for nine months until we are born.

The mother's body nourishes the child as you intended, providing milk to help it grow. You guide us with your kindness, sustain us with justice, and teach us through your wisdom. You give us life, and when the time comes, you take it away.

But if you destroy what you took such care to create, what was the purpose of making us in the first place?

I am speaking about all people, but even more, I am speaking about your chosen people. It breaks my heart to see their suffering, and I grieve for the people of Israel.

Now, I will begin to pray for myself and for others, because I see how much we have sinned in this world. I have also heard about the coming judgment. So, please, Lord my God, listen to my prayer as I speak to you.

The Seer's Prayer for The Divine Compassion on His People,

The prayer of Ezra before he was taken up:

Lord, you live forever, your throne has no limits, and your glory is beyond understanding. The mighty ones stand in fear before you, and at your command, they turn into fire and wind. Your words are true and unchanging, your commands are powerful, and your voice is terrifying.

You can dry up the deep waters with just a look, and your rebuke can make mountains melt. Your truth is clear for all to see. Please listen to your servant's voice, hear my prayer, and pay attention to my words.

As long as I live, I will speak, and as long as I have understanding, I will call out to you. Please do not focus on the sins of your people, but remember those who have served you faithfully. Do not hold onto the foolish actions of the wicked, but think of those who have kept your promises, even when they were treated with shame.

Do not judge those who have done evil before you, but remember those who have feared you with sincerity. Do not destroy those who have acted like animals, but instead look upon those who have followed the light of your law. Do not stay angry with those who have behaved worse than beasts, but love those who have always trusted in your glory.

We, along with those who came before us, have done wrong and acted foolishly. Yet because of our sins, you are called the Compassionate One. If you are willing to show mercy to us, even though we have no good deeds to offer, you will be known as the Gracious One.

The righteous who have done good already have their rewards stored with you. But what is a person that you should be so angry with them? Why be so harsh with a mortal race?

The truth is, there is no one who has not sinned, no one who has lived without doing wrong. So, Lord, let your kindness be known by showing mercy to those who have no good works to offer.

The Divine Reply

And he answered me, saying: Some of the things you have said are correct, and they will happen as you have spoken.

I do not focus on those who do evil, their death, their judgment, or their destruction. Instead, I take joy in the creation of the righteous, in their lives, and in the rewards they will receive.

For as you have said, so it will be.

Mankind Is Like Seed Sown (VIII. 41-45)

Just as a farmer plants many seeds and grows many plants, not all of them survive or take root. In the same way, not everyone who is born will live.

And I answered, "Lord, if I have found favor in your sight, may I ask something? A farmer's seeds will not grow unless they receive rain at the right time, and too much rain can even destroy them. But people are different—they were made by your own hands, in your own image, and you created everything for their sake. How can they be compared to seeds?

Please, Lord, have mercy on your people. Show kindness to your creation, for they belong to you, and you are full of compassion."

The Final Reply: Let the Seer Contemplate the Lot o The Blessed Which He Is Destined to Share (VIII. 46 62)

And he answered me, saying:

"The things of this world belong to those who live in it now, and the things of the future are for those who will come later. You cannot love my creation more than I do. But you have compared yourself to the wicked too many times—do not do this!

However, you will be honored before the Most High because you have humbled yourself, as you should, and have not tried to place yourself among the righteous. Because of this, you will be given even greater honor.

In the end, those who live on the earth will suffer greatly because of their pride. But instead of worrying about them, think about yourself and ask about the rewards of those who are like you.

For you, Paradise is open, the Tree of Life is planted, and the future world is prepared. A place of joy is waiting, a city has been built, and a peaceful rest has been set aside. All that is good has been made complete, and wisdom has reached its fullness. Evil has been locked away, sickness will no longer exist, death will disappear, the grave will be forgotten, and pain will be no more.

In the end, the treasures of life will be revealed. So do not ask again about those who will perish, because they were given freedom, but they rejected the Most High.

They scorned his law and worked to remove his ways from the earth. They even mistreated his faithful ones and said in their hearts, 'There is no God,' even though they knew they would die one day.

163

Just as the rewards I told you about are waiting for the righteous, suffering and torment are also prepared for the wicked. The Most High never wanted people to be destroyed, but they dishonored his name and refused to be grateful. They rejected the one who gave them life.

And so, my judgment is near. This is something I have not revealed to many people, but only to you and a few like you."

IX. The Signs of The End Reviewed (VIII. 63-IX. 63.

And I said, "Lord, you have shown me many signs of what will happen in the last days, but you haven't told me when it will happen."

He answered, "Pay close attention and think carefully. When you see that some of these signs have already happened, you will know that the Most High is preparing to visit the world He created.

When you notice earthquakes, crowds in chaos, people plotting against each other, leaders struggling for power, and rulers in confusion, understand that these are the events the Most High spoke about long ago.

Just like everything in the world has a clear beginning and end, the times set by the Most High are also known. Their beginnings come with warnings and signs of power, and their end will bring judgment and more signs.

Anyone who survives or escapes—whether through their actions or through their faith—will be safe from the dangers I have described. They will see my salvation in the land I have set apart forever.

But those who ignored my ways will be shocked, and those who rejected and abandoned them will suffer.

All who refused to recognize me while they were alive, even when

I was kind to them, and all who rejected my laws while they had the freedom to follow them, will realize the truth after death.

The Fewness of The Saved Further Justified

So don't focus on how the wicked will be punished. Instead, think about how the righteous will live—the ones for whom this world was created.

I replied, "I keep saying, and I will say it again, that more people will be lost than saved. It's like comparing the vast ocean waves to a tiny drop of water."

He answered, "Just as the land determines the kind of seeds that grow, and flowers decide their own colors, and work produces different smells, everything follows a pattern. The farmer's field matches his efforts.

Before people even existed, I had already prepared a place for them to live. No one could stop me—because no one was there yet.

Now that they are here, living in a stable world with everything they need and a law they cannot fully understand, they have become corrupt in their actions. I looked at my world and saw that it was ruined. I saw my creation and realized it was in danger because of the way people behaved.

So I decided to spare only a few. I saved one grape from a whole bunch and one plant from an entire forest.

Let the many be destroyed, since they were created for nothing. But let my chosen ones remain, for they are precious and took great effort to bring into existence.

Conclusion of The Vision

If you separate yourself for seven more days—but this time, do not fast—go to an open field full of flowers, where no buildings have been built. Eat only the flowers from the field. Do not eat meat or drink wine, only the flowers.

Pray with deep devotion to the Most High, and I will come to you and speak with you.

Introduction (IX. 26-28)

I went to the field called Arpad, just as he told me, and sat among the flowers. I ate the plants from the field, and they satisfied me.

After seven days, as I lay on the grass, I felt something stir in my heart again, just like before. Then my mouth opened, and I began to speak to the Most High.

The Glory of The Law and Israel: A Contrast (IX. 29-37)

And I said, "Lord, you truly showed yourself to our ancestors in the wilderness when they left Egypt. They traveled through a barren land where nothing grew and no one had ever lived.

You spoke to them, saying, 'Listen to me, Israel, and pay attention, descendants of Jacob! I am planting my Law within you, and it will grow and produce good things. Through it, you will be honored forever.'

But our ancestors received the Law and did not follow it. They were given commandments but did not obey them. The Law itself never faded because it belongs to you, but those who received it perished because they failed to live by it.

It's like how the earth receives seeds, or the sea holds a ship, or a container is filled with food—these things may be used up or destroyed, but what holds them remains. But for us, it has been different.

We received the Law, yet because of our sins, we are destroyed along with our hearts that once accepted it.

Still, your Law does not fade away. It remains in its full glory."

The Vision of The Disconsolate Woman
(IX. 38–X. 24)

As I was thinking about these things, I looked up and saw a woman on my right. She was crying loudly, deeply distressed, and sighing in sorrow. Her clothes were torn, and she had thrown dust on her head in grief.

I stopped thinking about my own concerns and turned to her, asking, "Why are you weeping? What is causing you such deep pain?"

She replied, "Please, my lord, allow me to cry freely and continue to grieve, for my heart is filled with sorrow, and I feel completely broken."

I said, "Tell me what has happened to you."

She answered, "I was unable to have children. For thirty years, I was married but could not conceive. Every single day and night, I prayed to the Most High, begging for a child.

Then, after those thirty years, God finally heard my prayers. He saw my suffering, understood my pain, and blessed me with a son.

I was overjoyed. My husband, my neighbors, and I all celebrated and praised the Mighty One. I raised my son with great effort and love.

When he grew up, I arranged for him to be married and planned a joyful wedding feast. But on the night of his wedding, as he entered his new home, he suddenly collapsed and died.

In my grief, I put out the lights, and the people in my town came to comfort me. But I remained silent, waiting until the next day and through the night.

Once everyone was asleep and thought I was resting too, I got up in the darkness, ran away, and came to this field where you see me now.

I have decided that I will never return to the city. I will not eat or drink, but I will continue to mourn and fast until I die."

I let go of my own thoughts and, in my frustration, said to her, "You are being more foolish than any other woman! Can't you see the suffering around us? Do you not realize what has happened to all of us?

Look at Zion, the mother of us all—she is in deep sorrow and has been humiliated beyond measure.

Yes, you grieve for your one son, but we grieve for an entire world in mourning.

Ask the earth, and she will tell you—she has witnessed the birth of countless people, and every one of them, from the beginning of time until now, has passed away. Many more will come, and they too will face destruction.

Who, then, should grieve more? You, for your one son, or the earth, which has lost countless lives?

And if you say, 'My grief is different because I lost the child I carried in my womb, the one I gave birth to and raised with love and hardship,'

Remember that the earth, just like a mother, has brought forth all of humanity. Every person who has ever lived was born from the earth, and all return to it.

So now, keep your sorrow within you. Face your pain with strength, and endure the hardship that has come upon you!"

If you accept the Most High's judgment as fair, then one day, you will be reunited with your son and be honored among women.

So go back to the city, return to your husband.

But she replied, "I will not go back. I will not return to the city or to my husband. I will stay here and die."

I continued speaking to her, saying, "No, don't do this! Instead, think about Zion's suffering and take comfort in Jerusalem's sorrow.

Look at what has happened—our sacred places are destroyed, our altars torn down, our Temple ruined. Our worship has ended, our songs have stopped, and our joy has faded. The light of our lamp has gone out, the ark of the covenant has been taken, and our holy places have been defiled.

The name we carry has been dishonored, our leaders have been shamed, our priests burned, and our Levites taken as prisoners. Our young women have been violated, our wives have been abused, our prophets captured, our watchmen scattered, our children enslaved, and our strongest warriors have been brought low.

And worst of all—the very symbol of Zion's glory has been taken away and handed over to those who hate us.

So let go of your overwhelming grief. Turn to the Mighty One so He may have mercy on you, and the Most High may give you rest from all your suffering."

Sion's Glory; The Vision of The Heavenly Jerusalem (X. 25 28)

As I was speaking with her, her face suddenly began to shine brightly, like a flash of lightning. I was terrified and too afraid to go near her, my heart filled with shock and confusion.

As I tried to understand what was happening, she suddenly let out a loud, terrifying cry, so powerful that the entire earth seemed to shake at the sound of her voice.

Then, as I looked again, she was gone. In her place, I saw a great city with strong, deep foundations. Fear took hold of me, and I cried out,

"Where is the angel Uriel, who has been with me since the beginning? He is the one who led me into this overwhelming experience. Now, I feel lost, my body weak, and my prayers seem worthless."

The Vision Interpreted (X. 29-57)

As I lay on the ground, feeling as if I were dead, the angel who had spoken to me before returned. He saw me there, weak and confused, and took my right hand. He helped me stand up and gave me strength. Then he asked,

"What is troubling you? Why are you so disturbed? Why is your mind so overwhelmed?"

I replied, "Because you left me! I did everything you told me—I went into the field, and I saw something beyond my understanding. I cannot explain it."

The angel said, "Stand up, and I will help you understand."

I said, "Please, my lord, speak to me, but do not leave me again, or I fear I will die too soon.

I have seen things I do not understand, and I have heard things that confuse me. Is my mind deceiving me? Am I only seeing a dream?

I beg you, my lord, explain this terrifying vision to me."

The angel answered, "Listen carefully, and I will teach you. I will reveal what you are afraid of, because the Most High has shared many secrets with you.

He has seen your righteous heart, how deeply you grieve for your people, and how much you mourn for Zion.

Now, here is the meaning of what you saw.

The woman who appeared to you in mourning—the one you tried to comfort—

She was not just a woman. She was Zion, the city you now see being built before you.

When she spoke of her son's misfortune, this is what it means:

The woman you saw is Zion itself, which has now become a great city.

When she told you she had been barren for thirty years, it represents the three thousand years before offerings were ever made there.

Then, after three thousand years, Solomon built the city and offered sacrifices in it. That is when the 'barren woman' finally bore a son.

When she spoke of raising her son with hardship, that represents the building and growth of Jerusalem.

When she said her son entered his wedding chamber and died, this symbolizes the fall and destruction of Jerusalem.

You saw how she mourned for her children, and you tried to

comfort her.

Now, the Most High has seen how deeply you grieve for Zion, how your heart is truly broken for her suffering.

Because of this, He has allowed you to see her future glory and her true beauty.

That is why I told you to wait for me in the field, where no houses were built.

I knew the Most High was about to reveal these things to you.

That is also why I brought you to a place with no buildings—because no human structure could remain where the City of the Most High was about to be revealed.

But do not be afraid. Let your heart be at peace.

Go forward and see the light of Zion's glory. Look at the greatness of her buildings, as far as your eyes can see.

Then, you will hear as much as your ears can take in.

You are blessed above many others, for the Most High has chosen you among only a few."

Transition To the Fifth Vision {X. 58-59)

But tomorrow night, you must stay here.

The Most High will show you a vision of the events that will take place on earth in the last days.

Vision V

(X. 60-XII. The Vision (X. 60---XII. Ja)

I stayed there that night, just as I was told.

The next night, I had a vision. I saw a huge eagle rising from the sea. It had twelve wings and three heads. As I watched, it spread its wings over the whole earth, and the winds from the sky blew around it. Clouds gathered toward it.

Then, I saw that smaller wings grew out of its large wings, but they were weak and unimportant. The eagle's heads remained still, but the middle head was larger than the others, even though it too was resting.

Then, the eagle commanded its wings to rule over the earth and its people. I saw that everything beneath the sky became subject to it, and no creature on earth resisted.

The eagle then stood on its claws and spoke to its wings, saying, "Go and rule over the earth. But rest now—do not all rise at once. Wake up at different times, and leave the heads for last."

I noticed that the eagle's voice did not come from its heads but from the middle of its body. I counted its small wings—there were eight.

Then, I saw one wing rise from the right side and rule over the earth. But after a while, it disappeared completely, leaving no trace.

Then, a second wing rose and ruled for a long time, but eventually, it too was destroyed like the first.

I heard a voice speaking to the second wing:

"You who have ruled for so long, listen! No ruler after you will hold power for as long as you did—not even for half as long."

Then, a third wing rose and ruled, just like the others, but it was also destroyed. The same happened to each of the wings—one after another, they ruled and then fell.

Later, I saw some of the smaller wings on the right side try to rule the earth. Some succeeded but were quickly destroyed. Others rose but never gained power.

Eventually, all twelve wings were gone, along with two of the small wings. All that remained of the eagle was its three resting heads and six small wings.

Then, I saw two of the small wings separate from the others and move under the right head, while the remaining four stayed in place.

I watched as these four small wings tried to rise to power. One of them succeeded but was quickly destroyed. The second tried, but it fell even faster than the first.

The last two small wings also thought they would rule, but before they could, something happened.

The middle head, which had been resting, suddenly woke up. It was larger than the other two heads.

It joined with the other two heads and turned on the last two small wings, devouring them before they could take power.

Then, the middle head ruled over the entire earth. It treated the people harshly and had more power than all the wings before it.

But suddenly, the middle head was destroyed, just like the wings had been.

Now, only the two remaining heads ruled over the earth and its people. Then, I saw the head on the right devour the head on the left, leaving only one.

Then, I heard a voice say, "Look ahead, Ezra, and see what happens at the end."

I looked and saw a lion coming out of the forest. It roared loudly, and then I heard it speak with a human voice. It spoke to the eagle, saying:

"Listen, eagle! I will tell you what the Most High says.

Are you not the one who remains from the…"

The Most High said, "I created four great beasts to rule over the world, and through them, the end of time would come.

You, the fourth beast, have risen above all the others before you. You have ruled over the earth with cruelty and have brought suffering to the whole world. You have lived among people for a long time, deceiving them and ruling unfairly.

You have stolen from the poor and mistreated those who are honest. You have harmed the humble, hated those who do what is right, and loved those who are deceitful. You have destroyed the homes of the successful and torn down the walls of those who never wronged you.

Because of your arrogance, your sins have reached the Most High.

Now, He has looked upon the times, and they have come to an end. The days He set in place have been fulfilled.

So, you, the eagle, will be completely destroyed—your great wings, your small and wicked wings, your cruel heads, your sharp claws, and your entire hateful body.

The earth will finally be at peace, free from violence. It will no longer suffer but will look forward to the judgment and mercy of its Creator."

Then, after the lion spoke these words to the eagle, I saw the last remaining head suddenly destroyed.

Then, the two wings that had tried to take power rose up to rule, but their rule was short and filled with chaos.

I watched as they too were destroyed, and the entire body of the eagle was burned. The earth stood in shock at what had happened.

The Interpretation Of The Vision (XII. 3B-39)

I woke up in great distress and fear and said to myself, "This is happening to me because I have been seeking to understand the ways of the Most High.

Now, I feel completely drained, my spirit is weak, and I have no strength left because of the overwhelming fear I experienced last night.

But I will pray to the Most High, and He will give me the strength to endure."

Then I prayed, "Lord, if I have found favor in your eyes, if you have truly blessed me above many others, and if my prayers have reached you,

Then strengthen me and help me understand this vision I have seen. Please explain it to me so that my soul may find peace.

Did you not choose me to reveal the end of times and the completion of these events?"

Then He answered me, saying, "This is the meaning of the vision you saw:

The eagle that rose from the sea represents the fourth kingdom, the same one your brother Daniel saw in his vision. However, it was not explained to him as I am explaining it to you now.

A time will come when a kingdom will rise on the earth, more powerful and terrifying than all the kingdoms before it.

Twelve kings will rule over it, one after another. But the second king will rule longer than the others.

This is the meaning of the twelve wings you saw.

As for the voice that spoke, not from the eagle's head but from the middle of its body, this means that during the middle of that kingdom's reign, it will face many divisions and nearly collapse. However, it will not fall at that time but will recover and continue to rule.

The eight small wings that grew under its larger wings represent eight kings who will rise within the kingdom. Their reigns will be short and their rule unstable. Two of them will die early, four will be saved for the final period, and two will remain until the very end.

The three resting heads you saw represent three powerful kings that the Most High will bring at the end of this kingdom's time. They will change many things and will oppress the world and its people with even more cruelty than those before them.

That is why they are called the heads of the eagle—because they will bring its final wickedness before its end.

The one large head that was destroyed means that one of these kings will die naturally, though he will still suffer.

As for the two remaining kings, they will be killed by the sword. One will destroy the other, but in the end, he too will fall by the sword.

The two wings that moved to the head on the right side represent those whom the Most High has set apart for the final moments. Their rule will be short and filled with chaos, just as you saw.

The lion that came from the forest, roaring and speaking to the eagle, correcting it for its wickedness—this represents the Messiah.

The Most High has kept Him for the final days. He will come from the line of David and will confront the rulers of this world. He will call them out for their evil, expose their corruption, and show them their sins.

He will bring them before God for judgment while they are still alive. After He rebukes them, He will destroy them.

But He will show mercy to my people, those who have remained faithful and stayed within my borders. He will bring them joy until the final Day of Judgment arrives, just as I have told you before.

This is the vision you saw, and this is its meaning.

You alone have been chosen to understand this mystery of the Most High.

So write down everything you have seen in a book and keep it in a safe place.

Teach it only to those among your people who are wise and have the understanding to keep these secrets.

But you must remain here for seven more days, for the Most High will reveal even more to you."

Conclusion Of the Vision (XII. 39B-48)

Then he left me.

When the people saw that seven days had passed and I had not returned to the city, they all gathered together—young and old—and came to me. They asked,

"What have we done wrong? How have we sinned against you that you have abandoned us and chosen to stay out here?

You are the last prophet left to us, like the last bunch of grapes from the harvest, like a light in the darkness, like a safe harbor for a ship caught in a storm.

Are all the troubles we have suffered not enough? Must we also lose you?

If you leave us too, then it would have been better if we had died when Zion was burned.

We are no better than those who perished there."

Hearing this, I cried out loudly and wept. Then I answered them,

"Have courage, Israel! Do not be discouraged, House of Jacob.

The Most High remembers you, and the Mighty One will not forget you forever.

I have not abandoned you, and I never will.

I came here to pray for the destruction of Zion and to ask for mercy for our Sanctuary, which has been humiliated."

Vision VI

(THE MAN FROM THE SEA)

(XIII. I-58)

The Vision (XIII. 1-13a)

After seven days, I had a vision in the night. I saw a powerful wind rise from the sea, stirring up massive waves.

Then, from deep within the sea, a figure like a man appeared. He flew through the sky on the clouds of heaven. Everywhere he looked, the earth trembled before him. When he spoke, those who heard his voice melted away like wax in a fire.

Then, I saw an enormous army gathering from all directions, coming together to fight against the man who had risen from the sea.

I watched as he carved out a massive mountain for himself and stood on top of it. I wanted to see where the mountain had come from, but I couldn't find its source.

Even though the armies were terrified, they still prepared to fight him.

But he didn't raise his hand, pick up a spear, or use any weapon of war. Instead, he opened his mouth, and streams of fire, powerful winds, and burning coals poured out.

The fire, wind, and stormy flames combined and struck the army with overwhelming force. The entire multitude was instantly burned up, leaving nothing behind but ashes and smoke. I was shocked at what I saw.

Then, the man came down from the mountain and called out to another group of people, who peacefully came to him.

Many people approached him—some happy, some sad. Some were in chains, while others brought those who were to be offered.

At this point, I woke up in great distress. I prayed to the Most High and said,

"Lord, from the beginning, you have shown me these great wonders. Even though I am unworthy, you have answered my prayers.

Now, please reveal the meaning of this vision to me.

I fear for those who will be left alive in those days, but even more for those who will not survive.

Those who do not live to see these events will mourn what they have missed.

But those who do survive will suffer greatly, facing extreme dangers and hardships, as these visions have shown.

Yet, it is better to endure and witness these things than to disappear like a cloud and never see how the end of time unfolds."

Then He answered me, saying,

"I will explain your vision and also tell you about the people you have asked about.

As for those who survive and those who do not—here is the meaning:

Whoever endures the dangers of that time will be saved, as will those who have remained faithful and lived righteously before the Most High.

So know this—those who survive will receive more blessings than those who have died."

L. THE APOCALYPSE OF EZRA
THE INTERPRETATION OF THE VISION
(XIII. 25-53A)

Here is what your vision means:

The man you saw rising from the sea is the one the Most High has been keeping for a long time. He will come to save creation and bring to safety those who remain.

The fire, storm, and breath that came from his mouth—without the use of weapons—destroying the army that gathered to fight him, means this:

The time is coming when the Most High will rescue those on earth. A great terror will fall upon the people.

Nations will turn against each other—cities against cities, places against places, people against people, and kingdoms against kingdoms.

When these signs take place, just as I told you before, my Son will be revealed—the same man you saw rising from the sea.

When people hear his voice, they will abandon their battles and conflicts.

Then, as you saw, an uncountable number of people will gather to fight against him.

But he will stand on Mount Zion, and Zion itself will appear before everyone—fully prepared and built, just as you saw the mountain that was not made by human hands.

My Son will confront these people for their wickedness, like a storm striking against them.

He will reveal all their evil deeds and the punishment they are about to face.

Then, like a blazing fire, he will destroy them effortlessly—by the Law of the One who is like fire.

The peaceful people he gathered afterward are the nine and a half tribes who were taken from their land during the time of King Josiah.

The Assyrian King Salmanassar captured them and took them to the other side of the Euphrates River, exiling them to a distant land.

But they made a decision among themselves—to leave behind the other nations and go to a place where no people had ever lived before.

There, they hoped to keep the Law that they had failed to follow in their own land.

They traveled through the narrow paths of the Euphrates, and the Most High performed miracles for them.

He held back the river's waters until they had all crossed safely.

Their journey was long—it took a year and a half—until they reached a place called Arsaph, at the farthest edge of the world.

They have lived there until the end times.

But when their return is near, the Most High will once again stop the flow of the Euphrates, so they can cross back.

That is why you saw a great gathering of people coming in peace.

The people from your own nation who remain within my sacred land will also survive.

When my Son destroys the gathered armies, he will protect those who are left, and then he will show them many wonders.

I then asked, "Lord, why did I see the man coming from the sea?"

He answered, "Just as no one can search the deep sea or fully know what lies beneath, no one on earth can see my Son or those with him—except in the time of his coming.

This is the meaning of your vision."

Transition To the Seventh Vision (XIII. 53B-58)

These things have been revealed to you alone

because you have set aside your own concerns and dedicated yourself to understanding the ways of the Most High. You have sought to learn the truths of the Law.

You have lived wisely and have treated understanding as your guide, like a mother who teaches her child.

That is why I have shown you these things—because the Most High has a reward for you.

In three days, I will speak to you again and reveal even greater wonders.

Then I went out into the field, walking for a long time, praising the Most High for the amazing things He has done throughout history.

I thanked Him for how He controls time and everything that happens within it.

And I stayed there for three days.

Vision VII

(Ch. Xiv)

Ezra's Commission (XIV. 1-17)

After this, as I was sitting under an oak tree, a voice suddenly came from a bush in front of me.

It called out, "Ezra, Ezra!"

I answered, "Here I am!" and stood up.

The voice said, "I revealed myself from a bush and spoke with Moses when my people were enslaved in Egypt.

I sent him to lead my people out of Egypt, through the wilderness, and up to Mount Sinai. I kept him near me for many days,

showing him great wonders, revealing the secrets of time, and explaining how everything would come to an end.

I told him that some of these words must be kept secret, while others should be shared.

Now I say the same to you, Ezra.

The signs I have shown you, the visions you have seen, and the explanations you have heard—keep them in your heart and hide them.

Because you will be taken away from this world, and you will stay with my Son and others like you until the end of time.

This world is growing old, and its time is almost over.

So, put your life in order, warn your people, comfort those who are struggling, and guide the wise.

Let go of this temporary life,

free yourself from the concerns of this world, stop worrying about death, and cast away all weakness.

Do not let these thoughts trouble you—leave these times behind!

Because the troubles you have already seen will be followed by even greater ones.

As the world ages, evil will increase, and suffering will spread among its people.

Truth will fade, and lies will take over.

Look! The great eagle you saw in your vision is already on its way."

Ezra Prays for Inspiration (XIV. R8-26)

I answered and said, "Lord, please let me speak!

I will do as you have commanded and warn the people who are alive now. But what about those who have not yet been born? Who will warn them?

The world is covered in darkness, and its people have no light.

The Law has been burned, and no one knows the works you have done or what you are about to do.

If I have found favor in your eyes, Lord, send your Holy Spirit to me. I will write down everything that has happened in the world from the very beginning—everything written in your Law—so that people may find the right path and those who live in the last days will know the way.

He answered and said, "Go, gather your people, and tell them not to look for you for forty days.

Prepare many writing tablets, and take with you Seraia, Daria, Shelemia, Helkana, and Shiel—these five men, because they are skilled in writing quickly.

Come here, and I will place a light of understanding in your heart that will not go out until you have finished writing.

When you are done, you will share some of what you write with everyone, but some you must keep hidden and give only to the wise.

Tomorrow at this time, you will begin writing."

Ezra's Last Words (XIV. 27-36)

I went and did as I was commanded, gathering all the people together and saying to them:

"Listen, Israel, to these words.

Our ancestors were once strangers in the land of Egypt, but they were rescued from there.

They received the Law of life, but they did not follow it. And just like them, you have also broken it.

You were given the land of Zion as an inheritance, but you and your ancestors sinned and did not follow the ways that Moses, the servant of the Lord, commanded you.

So the Most High, who is a fair judge, took away what had been given to you for a time.

Now, you are suffering here, and your brothers and sisters have

186

been scattered to a faraway land.

But if you turn back to the truth, discipline your hearts, and live rightly, you will be saved. And after death, you will receive mercy.

For after death, there will be judgment, and we will live again. Then, the names of the righteous will be honored, and the sins of the wicked will be exposed.

Until then, do not come near me or try to find me for forty days."

The Restoration of The Scriptures
(XIV. 37-48)

I took the five men, just as I was commanded, and we went into the field, where we stayed.

The next day, a voice called out to me, saying, "Ezra, open your mouth and drink what I give you."

I opened my mouth and saw a full cup coming toward me. It looked like it was filled with water, but its appearance was like fire. I took the cup and drank from it.

As soon as I drank, my heart was filled with understanding, my mind overflowed with wisdom, and my spirit held onto knowledge. My mouth opened, and I could not stop speaking.

The Most High gave the five men the ability to understand, and they wrote down everything I spoke, using writing they had never known before.

I stayed there for forty days. During the day, I spoke, and they wrote. At night, they ate bread, but I remained awake, never stopping.

By the end of forty days, we had written ninety-four books.

When the forty days were over, the Most High spoke to me and said,

"The first twenty-four books you have written, make public. Let both those who are worthy and those who are not read them.

But keep the other seventy books hidden, and give them only to the wise among your people.

For in these books are the deep secrets of understanding, the sources of wisdom, and the path to knowledge."

I followed the command exactly, in the seventh year, during the sixth week, five thousand years after creation, on the twelfth day of the third month.

Conclusion Of the Book (XIV. 49-50)

After writing everything down, Ezra was taken away to be with others like him.

He was forever known as the Scribe of the Knowledge of the Most High.

This was the conclusion of Ezra's first account.

The Apocalypse of Paul

Introduction

The Acts of Paul and Thecla is an ancient Christian text from the second century that tells the story of Thecla, a noble young woman from Iconium, and how her life changed after meeting the Apostle Paul. Although it is part of a larger work called the Acts of Paul, this story became well-known on its own because of its exciting events and powerful themes.

In the story, Thecla is deeply moved by Paul's teachings about remaining pure and the promise of resurrection. She decides to leave her arranged marriage and go against her family's wishes to follow him. Because of her strong faith, she faces many dangers, including being sentenced to death by fire and thrown into an arena with wild animals. However, she miraculously survives each trial. In one striking moment, she even baptizes herself, showing her independence and deep belief in God.

This text also includes one of the earliest descriptions of Paul. He is described as a man of average height, with little hair, slightly bent legs, and large eyes. His eyebrows met in the middle, his nose was long, and he was known for his kindness and grace.

Scholars believe the Acts of Paul and Thecla was written sometime in the second century, possibly as early as 68–98 AD. A church leader named Tertullian later mentioned that a priest from Asia was removed from his position for writing it, showing that the text was seen as controversial in early Christian communities.

The story has had a lasting impact, especially in discussions about women's roles in the early church. Thecla's journey highlights themes of female strength, devotion, and the struggles faced by women who chose faith over traditional expectations. Her role as a preacher and baptizer has led to debates about whether women had leadership positions in early Christianity.

Even though the Acts of Paul and Thecla is not part of the official New Testament, it provides important insight into early Christian beliefs, the respect given to female figures, and the way gender and authority worked in ancient religious communities.

The Acts of Paul

As Paul traveled to Iconium after escaping from Antioch, he was accompanied by Demas and Hermogenes. These two men acted as if they were devoted followers, but they were not sincere. Paul, however, focused only on the goodness of Christ and did not treat them badly. Instead, he showed them kindness and spoke to them about Jesus, sharing details about His birth, resurrection, and the great things Christ had revealed to him.

A man named Onesiphorus heard that Paul was coming to Iconium. Wanting to welcome him, he went out with his wife Lectra and their children, Silas and Zeno. Titus had described what Paul looked like since Onesiphorus had never seen him in person, only in visions. He stood along the road to Lystra, watching travelers carefully, searching for Paul based on the description.

Then he saw Paul approaching. Paul was a small man, bald, with bowed legs, a strong build, thick eyebrows that met in the middle, and a long nose. But more than his appearance, he carried a presence full of grace—sometimes he looked like an ordinary man, and other times, his face shone like an angel's. When Paul saw Onesiphorus, he smiled.

Onesiphorus greeted him, saying, "Welcome, servant of the blessed God!"

Paul replied, "May grace be with you and your family."

Demas and Hermogenes, jealous of the special greeting, tried to act more devoted than they really were. Demas asked, "Are we not also servants of the blessed God? Why didn't you greet us the same way?"

Onesiphorus responded, "I do not see in you the actions of righteous men. But if you are truly faithful, you are welcome in my home as well."

Paul went into Onesiphorus' house, and everyone was filled with joy. They prayed together, broke bread, and Paul spoke about self-control and resurrection. He shared teachings such as:

"Blessed are those with pure hearts, for they will see God.

Blessed are those who keep their bodies pure, for they will be a home for God's spirit.

Blessed are those who practice self-control, for God will guide them.

Blessed are those who do not chase after worldly pleasures, for they will be called righteous.

Blessed are those who are married but remain devoted to God, for He will be their greatest reward.

Blessed are those who respect and honor the Lord, for they will be like angels.

Blessed are those who stay true to their baptism, for they will find peace with the Father and the Son.

Blessed are those who show kindness and mercy, for they will receive the same and will not suffer in judgment.

Blessed are those who remain pure, for they are pleasing to God and will not lose their reward.

The word of the Father will save them when His Son comes, and they will live in peace forever."

As Paul spoke in the church gathered at Onesiphorus' house, a young woman named Thecla sat by a nearby window, listening intently. She was the daughter of Theocleia and had been promised in marriage to a man named Thamyris. But as she heard Paul's teachings about purity and prayer, she was captivated, staying by the window day and night without looking away. She was deeply drawn to the faith and filled with joy as she listened.

When she saw many other women gathering to hear Paul, her desire grew stronger. She longed to be counted among them, to stand in Paul's presence, and to hear the message of Christ directly from him. Though she had never seen him before, his words alone had already touched her heart.

Thecla stayed by the window, listening intently, refusing to move. Seeing this, her mother, Theocleia, sent for Thamyris, her fiancé. Thamyris arrived happily, expecting to see Thecla, thinking their marriage would happen soon.

Theocleia turned to him and said, "Thamyris, I have something strange to tell you. For three days and nights, Thecla has not left the window. She refuses to eat or drink and keeps staring outside, as if she's watching something fascinating. She has become completely captivated by a foreign man who teaches strange ideas. I can't understand why my daughter, who has always been so modest, is behaving this way.

This man is dangerous—he is turning the whole city against our ways, including your Thecla. Both women and young men are going to listen to him, learning to fear God and live in purity. My daughter is trapped by his words like a spider in a web. She listens to everything he says with incredible focus, as if under a spell. Please, go talk to her— she is supposed to be your wife."

Thamyris approached Thecla, kissed her, and tried to hide his concern. "Thecla, my love, why are you sitting here like this? What has come over you? Look at me! Remember our engagement and be ashamed of this behavior."

Her mother also pleaded, "My child, why do you just sit there in silence, staring, acting as if you have lost your mind?"

They both cried—Thamyris, fearing he had lost his bride, and Theocleia, feeling as if she had lost her daughter. Even the servants grieved for their mistress, and the entire house was filled with sorrow. But Thecla didn't react. She didn't turn away from the window. She kept listening to Paul's words.

Frustrated, Thamyris stormed out into the street, watching people come and go from Paul's gathering. He spotted two men arguing and called out to them. "Tell me, who is this man leading people astray? He is deceiving young men and keeping women from getting married! If you can tell me who he is, I will pay you well—I am a wealthy and important man in this city."

Demas and Hermogenes, who had been pretending to follow Paul, saw an opportunity. "We don't know exactly who he is," they said, "but he tells people not to marry. He teaches that there is no true resurrection except for those who remain pure and do not corrupt their bodies."

Thamyris invited them to his house for a feast, serving them fine food and plenty of wine. He wanted to win them over so they would help him get Thecla back. As they ate, he asked, "Tell me about this man's teachings. I need to understand. I am deeply troubled because Thecla is obsessed with him, and I cannot marry her because of it."

Demas and Hermogenes gave him a plan. "Take him to the governor, Castelios. Accuse him of convincing people to follow new Christian beliefs, and the governor will deal with him quickly. Then you will be able to marry Thecla. We can also explain the so-called 'resurrection' he speaks of—it has already happened in our children. We were 'reborn' when we came to know the true God."

Hearing this, Thamyris was furious. The next morning, he gathered city leaders, public officials, and an angry crowd. Carrying clubs, they marched to Onesiphorus' house and shouted, "You have corrupted the people of Iconium! You have turned Thecla against me, and now she refuses to marry. Let's take him to the governor!"

The crowd chanted, "Away with this magician! He has tricked our wives and convinced many to change their beliefs!"

Thamyris stood before the governor and shouted, "This man is dangerous! He convinces young women to avoid marriage. Let him explain to you why he teaches these things!"

Demas and Hermogenes whispered to Thamyris, "Say that he is a Christian. That will be enough to get rid of him."

The governor, however, decided to question Paul directly. "Who are you?" he asked. "And what exactly do you teach? These men are accusing you of serious things."

Paul raised his voice and answered, "If you want to know what I teach, listen carefully. I serve the one true God, who is just and powerful. He does not need anything, but He cares about saving people. He sent me to lead them away from sin, corruption, and death, so they can live in holiness. That is why God sent His Son—whom I preach—to bring hope to the lost. He came to rescue the world from judgment, so that instead of punishment, people could have faith, fear God, live in holiness, and love the truth.

If this is what I teach, how am I doing anything wrong?"

The governor listened but was unsure of what to do. Instead of making a decision right away, he ordered Paul to be arrested and put in prison. "I will question him more when I have time," he said.

Late at night, Thecla took off her bracelets and gave them to the gatekeeper in exchange for letting her through. Once inside, she gave the jailer a silver mirror so she could visit Paul. She sat at his feet, listening to him speak about the greatness of God. Paul remained fearless, trusting completely in God, and Thecla's faith grew stronger. Moved by what she heard, she kissed the chains he was wearing.

Meanwhile, Thecla's family was searching for her. Thamyris, her fiancé, ran through the streets in a panic, asking where she had gone. One of the gatekeeper's fellow servants told them she had left during the night. When they questioned the gatekeeper himself, he admitted, "She went to see the foreigner in the prison."

They rushed to the prison and found Thecla sitting beside Paul, completely focused on his words. It was as if she were bound to him, not by chains, but by devotion. Furious, they gathered a crowd and reported everything to the governor. He immediately ordered Paul to be brought before him.

Thecla, however, remained where she was, lying on the ground where Paul had taught her. The governor then ordered her to be brought forward as well. But instead of fear, Thecla was filled with joy.

When Paul was brought before the crowd, people shouted angrily, "He is a magician! Get rid of him!" But the governor was curious and wanted to hear what Paul had to say about Christ. Afterward, he turned to Thecla and asked, "Why have you not obeyed Thamyris and followed the laws of Iconium?"

Instead of responding, Thecla kept her eyes on Paul. Seeing her silence, her mother became enraged and shouted, "Burn this disgraceful girl! If she refuses to marry, let her be burned in the theater! Let all women see what happens to those who listen to this man!"

The governor was deeply troubled. He ordered Paul to be beaten and thrown out of the city, and he sentenced Thecla to be burned. The crowd rushed to the theater, eager to see the punishment. Thecla, however, only looked around for Paul, like a lamb searching for its shepherd. As she scanned the crowd, she saw someone who looked like Paul sitting there. She said to herself, Even though I must face this, Paul has come to see me. She kept her eyes on him until, suddenly, he disappeared into the sky.

The servants and young women gathered wood to build the fire for her execution. As Thecla was led in, stripped of her clothes, the governor was moved to tears. Even as she stood there, about to be burned, he was amazed by the strength she carried within her.

The executioners prepared the fire, and Thecla made the sign of the cross before stepping onto the wood. The flames were lit, and a huge fire blazed around her. But miraculously, it never touched her. God showed her mercy—there was a sudden earthquake, and dark clouds covered the sky. A powerful storm brought down heavy rain and hail, pouring over the fire and putting it out. Many in the crowd were injured by the storm, but Thecla was unharmed.

Meanwhile, Paul had left Iconium with Onesiphorus, his wife, and children. They were fasting as they traveled toward Daphne. After several days without food, the children complained, "Paul, we are hungry, but we have no money to buy bread."

Onesiphorus had given up all his possessions to follow Paul, so they had nothing left. Paul took off his cloak and said, "Go, child, sell this and buy some bread."

As the boy went to buy food, he saw Thecla nearby and was stunned. "Thecla! Where are you going?"

She answered, "I survived the fire and am looking for Paul."

The boy excitedly told her, "Come with me! He has been praying for you for six days, worrying about what happened."

When Thecla arrived at the place where Paul was, he was kneeling in prayer, saying, "Lord Jesus, keep Thecla safe from the fire and protect her, for she belongs to You."

Hearing his words, Thecla cried out, "Father of heaven and earth, I bless You! You saved me so that I could find Paul again."

Paul stood up, saw her, and lifted his hands in praise. "God, who knows our hearts, Father of Jesus Christ, I bless You! You have answered my prayers so quickly."

They shared five loaves of bread, some herbs, and water, rejoicing in the works of Christ. Then Thecla turned to Paul and said, "I will cut my hair and follow you wherever you go."

But Paul cautioned her, "The world is cruel, and you are a beautiful young woman. I worry that you might face even greater challenges than before and might not be able to withstand them."

Thecla insisted, "Just baptize me in Christ, and no temptation will overcome me."

Paul responded, "Thecla, be patient. In time, you will receive baptism."

Paul then sent Onesiphorus and his family back to Iconium, while he and Thecla traveled to Antioch. As they entered the city, a powerful leader named Alexander saw Thecla and became infatuated with her. He tried to bribe Paul with gifts, hoping to win her over.

Paul, wanting to protect her, simply said, "I don't know the woman you're speaking of. She is not mine."

But Alexander was determined. He grabbed Thecla in the street, trying to claim her for himself. Thecla fought back, pushing him away. She called out, "Do not touch a servant of God! I am a noblewoman from Iconium, and because I refused to marry Thamyris, I was cast out of my city!"

She tore Alexander's cloak and knocked off the crown he wore on his head, humiliating him in public.

Embarrassed and angry, Alexander dragged her before the governor and accused her of attacking him. The governor asked if this was true, and Thecla admitted, "Yes, I did those things."

Hearing this, the governor sentenced her to be thrown to wild animals. Women in the crowd were shocked and shouted, "This is unfair! This is a cruel judgment!"

A noblewoman named Tryphaena, whose daughter Falconilla had died, felt sympathy for Thecla and took her in, treating her with kindness.

When the time came for her to face the wild animals, the soldiers tied Thecla to a fierce lioness, but instead of attacking her, the lioness lay down at her feet and licked them. The crowd watching was amazed.

The next day, they sent in more wild beasts, and Thecla stood, stretching her hands toward heaven in prayer. When she finished, she saw a pool of water nearby and said, Now is the time for me to baptize myself.

Ignoring the crowd's warnings, she jumped into the water, declaring, "In the name of Jesus Christ, I baptize myself!"

At that moment, lightning flashed, and the seals in the water died. A cloud of fire surrounded Thecla, covering her body so that no one could see her nakedness. The wild beasts could not come near her, and once again, she was saved.

As more wild animals were released into the arena, the women in the crowd wept. Some threw fragrant herbs like nard and cassia, filling the air with sweet scents. Yet, none of the animals touched Thecla. It was as if they had fallen into a deep sleep.

Frustrated, Alexander turned to the governor and said, "I have fierce bulls that will surely kill her. Let's tie her to them."

The governor, looking troubled, replied, "Do as you wish."

They tied Thecla's feet between two bulls and placed burning hot irons beneath them to make the animals panic and attack. The bulls ran wildly, but instead of harming her, the flames burned through the ropes, freeing Thecla completely.

Meanwhile, Tryphaena, who had been watching, fainted from shock. The people cried out, "Queen Tryphaena is dead!" Chaos spread through the city, and the governor ordered the games to stop.

Alexander, now afraid of the consequences, begged the governor, "Please have mercy on me and the city. Let this woman go. If Caesar hears about what happened, he will punish us, especially since Queen

Tryphaena has just collapsed beside the arena!"

The governor then called Thecla and asked, "Who are you? Why have none of the animals harmed you?"

Thecla answered, "I am a servant of the living God. I believe in His Son, in whom He is pleased. That is why no animal has touched me. He alone brings salvation and eternal life. He is a refuge for those in trouble, a comfort to the suffering, and hope for the lost. Those who do not believe in Him will not have eternal life."

The governor, amazed by her words, ordered her to be given clothes and allowed her to dress.

As she put on the garments, Thecla said, "The one who protected me while I was naked among the wild beasts will also clothe you with salvation on the day of judgment."

The governor then made an official announcement: "I release Thecla, a servant of God, who fears the Lord."

The women in the crowd cheered, shouting, "There is only one God—the God of Thecla!" Their voices were so powerful that the very foundations of the theater shook.

When Tryphaena heard the news, she rushed to meet Thecla and said, "Now I believe in the resurrection! Now I believe my daughter is alive! Come with me, and I will give you everything I have."

Thecla went with her and stayed in her home for eight days, teaching her about God. Even many of the servants in the household came to believe, and there was great joy.

After that, Thecla began searching for Paul and learned that he was in Myra, a city in Lycia. She dressed herself in a simple cloak, gathered a group of young men and women, and traveled there.

When she arrived, she found Paul preaching. Seeing her, Paul was surprised and worried, thinking she had been put on trial again. But Thecla ran to him and said, "Paul, I have received my baptism! The same God who worked through you for the Gospel has also worked in me for my baptism."

Paul took her to the home of a man named Hermæus, where she told him everything that had happened. Those who heard her story were amazed and encouraged. They all gathered in prayer for Tryphaena.

Then Thecla said, "I am going back to Iconium."

Paul blessed her, saying, "Go, and continue spreading the word of God."

Before she left, Tryphaena gave her many gifts, including fine clothes and gold. Thecla, in turn, gave much of it to Paul for helping the poor.

When she arrived in Iconium, she went straight to the house of Onesiphorus, where she had first heard Paul teach. She fell to the ground where Paul used to sit, crying as she prayed:

"God of this house, where You first shined Your light on me… Jesus Christ, Son of the living God, You were with me in the fire, You saved me from the wild beasts. May You always be glorified forever. Amen."

She discovered that Thamyris, her former fiancé, had died, but her mother was still alive. She sent for her mother and said, "Mother, do you now believe that the Lord rules in heaven? If you desire wealth, He has given it to you through me. If you desire your child, here I am beside you."

After speaking to her, Thecla left for Seleucia, where she lived in a cave for seventy-two years. She survived on herbs and water, sharing the word of God with many people.

However, some men in the city, who followed Greek beliefs and worked as doctors, became jealous of her. They saw how she healed the sick through faith, and since people no longer came to them for help, they wanted to get rid of her. They decided to send wicked men to attack her, believing that if she was harmed, she would lose her ability to heal.

But God protected her. As the men approached her cave, a rock suddenly opened, allowing Thecla to escape inside. The cave then closed behind her, leaving the men outside, unable to reach her. They only managed to tear a small piece of her veil.

Thecla then traveled to Rome, hoping to see Paul, but when she arrived, she found that he had already passed away. She stayed there for a short time before peacefully passing away herself.

Thecla was first thrown into the fire when she was seventeen and faced the wild beasts at eighteen. She lived in the cave for seventy-two years, dedicating her life to God. In total, she lived for ninety years. After healing many and spreading the Gospel, she passed away on September 24, resting among the saints in Christ Jesus. To Him be all glory and power forever. Amen.

The Book of Revelation of Peter

Many people will claim to be prophets, but they will spread false teachings that lead others down the wrong path. These false teachers will bring destruction upon themselves.

Then God will come to those who remain faithful—those who long for righteousness, endure hardships, and keep their souls pure in this life. He will bring justice against those who live in wickedness.

The Lord then said, "Let's go up to the mountain and pray."

So we, the twelve disciples, followed him. We asked him to show us one of our righteous brothers who had passed away, so we could understand what they were like. We hoped this would give us courage and help us inspire others to believe in our message.

As we prayed, two men suddenly appeared before the Lord, facing the east. Their faces shone as brightly as the sun, and their clothes sparkled with a brilliance beyond anything we had ever seen. Their beauty and glory were indescribable, and we could barely look at them.

We stared in amazement. Their bodies were whiter than the purest snow, yet at the same time, they had a soft red glow, like the petals of the most vibrant rose. The red and white blended perfectly, making them look even more magnificent.

Their curly hair shimmered and flowed over their shoulders like a crown made of fragrant flowers. It reminded me of a rainbow stretching across the sky. Their presence was breathtaking.

They had appeared so suddenly that we were left in complete awe.

I turned to the Lord and asked, "Who are these men?"

He answered, "These are your righteous brothers, the ones you wanted to see."

Then I asked, "Where do all the righteous live? What kind of place is it that gives them such beauty and glory?"

The Lord then revealed a vast and radiant land beyond this world. It was brighter than anything I had ever imagined, filled with pure light, as if the sun itself shone from within it. The air glowed with warmth, and the ground was covered in flowers that never faded, releasing a sweet and refreshing fragrance.

This land was full of beautiful, everlasting plants and trees that produced the most blessed fruit. Even from a distance, the scent of this paradise reached us, filling the air with its heavenly aroma.

The people in this place wore clothes as bright and beautiful as the robes of angels, matching the incredible beauty around them. Angels floated above, making the place even more breathtaking. Everyone there shared the same glory, and they sang together with one voice, praising God with joy.

The Lord said to us, "This is where your high priests and the righteous live."

But then, I saw another place—dark, filthy, and terrifying. It was a place of punishment. The air was thick and heavy, as gloomy as the dark clothing worn by both the punishing angels and those being punished. Some people were hanging by their tongues—these were the ones who had spoken against the righteous path. Beneath them, fire burned, causing them constant pain.

A huge lake of flaming mud was filled with people who had used righteousness for their own selfish gain. Tormenting angels caused them endless suffering. Nearby, women hung by their hair over the bubbling mud. They had dressed themselves to lure others into adultery. The men who had sinned with them hung by their feet, their heads sinking into the filthy, boiling mire.

I thought to myself, "I never imagined such a terrible place could exist."

I saw murderers and their accomplices thrown into a cramped space filled with venomous snakes. The snakes bit them over and over, making them twist and writhe in pain. Dark, crawling worms covered them like a thick cloud, adding to their suffering. The souls of the people they had killed stood nearby, watching and saying, "O God, your judgment is fair."

Not far from there, I saw another tight space where blood and filth from the suffering people drained into a pool, forming a lake. Women sat in the filthy liquid, submerged up to their necks. Across from them sat the children they had conceived but aborted. The children cried out, and sparks of fire shot from their mouths, burning the women's eyes. These were the women who had caused abortions and were now cursed for their actions.

Elsewhere, men and women burned up to their waists in a dark place while evil spirits beat them. Worms ate them from the inside, never stopping. These were the ones who had betrayed and attacked the righteous.

Nearby, some men and women chewed on their own lips in torment while burning irons were pressed into their eyes. They had spoken against righteousness and spread lies. Others bit their own tongues, and fire shot from their mouths—these were the false witnesses.

In another part of this place, sharp, burning-hot stones, sharper than swords, covered the ground. Men and women dressed in torn, dirty clothes rolled on them, suffering without end. These were the rich people who had put their trust in wealth, ignored orphans and widows, and disobeyed God's commands.

In a huge, bubbling lake filled with blood and filth, people stood knee-deep in the disgusting mixture. These were the greedy lenders who charged others unfair amounts of interest.

Others were thrown off a high cliff. When they hit the ground, they were forced to climb back up, only to be thrown down again, never finding rest. These were the men who had dishonored their bodies by acting like women and the women who had lain with each other like a man and woman should.

Next to the cliff, fire burned where men who had made idols for themselves stood, trapped in the flames. Nearby, other men and women carried rods, striking each other over and over without end.

In another place, men and women burned and twisted in agony. Their bodies roasted in the flames. These were the ones who had abandoned God's way to chase after their own selfish desires.

Thank You for Reading

Dear Reader,

We hope this timeless classic has sparked your imagination and enriched your literary journey. Now that you've turned the final page, we want to share a vision for the future of reading—one where every classic you've ever wanted to explore is at your fingertips, in a format that best suits your life.

We'd like to invite you to gain immediate, unlimited digital & audiobook access to hundreds of the most treasured literary classics ever written—along with the option to secure deluxe paperback, hardcover & box set editions at printing cost. Together, we can spark a new global literary renaissance alongside our small, independent publishing house called "The Library of Alexandria."

Thousands of years ago, the Library of Alexandria stood as a beacon of knowledge—until it was lost to history. We aim to reignite that spirit of preservation and discovery right now, in the modern age—only this time, it's accessible to all, in every language and every format.

Picture a world where every timeless classic, novel, poem, or philosophical treatise is not only available to read but also updated for today's readers—modernized, translated into any language or dialect, and ready to enjoy in any format you choose, whether that is in an eBook, audiobook, paperback, or deluxe hardcover & box set version a printing cost.

By joining our movement to rebuild the modern Library of Alexandria, you become part of an unprecedented mission to offer:

- **Unlimited Audiobook & eBook Access to the Greatest Classics of All Time**

  Instantly explore thousands of legendary works, from Plato and Shakespeare to Jane Austen and Leo Tolstoy. All are instantly ready to read or listen to, giving you a complete literary universe at your fingertips.

- **Paperback & Deluxe Editions at Printing Costs:**

  Purchase any title in a paperback, deluxe hardbound, or deluxe boxset edition at printing costs, shipped right to your doorstep. Curate your personal library of Alexandria with editions worthy of display—crafted to last, designed to captivate, and delivered straight to your door.

- **Modern translations for Contemporary Readers in all languages and dialects**

  Discover a vast selection of classics reimagined in clear, current language—no more struggling with outdated phrases or obscure references. Next to the original versions, we aim to offer translations in as many languages and dialects as possible.

  As we continue our translation efforts and add new languages, readers everywhere can connect with these works as if they were written today. By bridging linguistic divides, you're contributing to ensuring that these timeless stories become more meaningful, accessible, and inspiring for people across the globe.

- **Your Personal Library of Alexandria:**

  Over the months and years, you'll curate a unique physical archive of classics—each volume a testament to your taste, curiosity, and love of knowledge. It's not just about owning books—it's about curating a cultural legacy you'll cherish and pass down for generations to come.

- **Join a Global Literary Renaissance:**

  Your support fuels an ongoing mission: allowing us to reinvest in offering deluxe print editions (including special boxsets) at their true cost, broaden the range of available formats and translations, and extend the reach of these works to new audiences worldwide. By joining today, you're not just preserving a legacy of masterpieces; you set in motion a powerful wave of literary accessibility.

  We are more than a publisher—we're a movement, and we can't do it alone. Your support lets us scale our mission, preserving and reimagining history's greatest works for tomorrow's readers.

Become a Torchbearer of knowledge.

Thank you for picking up this book and allowing us into your literary journey. As you turn the pages, know that you're part of something larger: a global effort to keep these stories alive, share their wisdom across borders and generations, and spark a true cultural revival for the modern era.

If this resonates with you—please consider taking the next step by visiting:

www.libraryofalexandria.com

With gratitude and a shared love of knowledge,

The Modern Library of Alexandria Team

Visit:

www.libraryofalexandria.com

Or scan the code below:

www.ingramcontent.com/pod-product-compliance
Lightning Source LLC
Chambersburg PA
CBHW011203090426
42742CB00019B/3389